MOSES AND
THE EXODUS

The Bible for School and Home

by J. Paterson Smyth

The Bible for School and Home

MOSES AND
THE EXODUS

by

J. Paterson Smyth

YESTERDAY'S CLASSICS

ITHACA, NEW YORK

This edition, first published in 2017 by Yesterday's Classics, an imprint of Yesterday's Classics, LLC, is an unabridged republication of the text originally published by Sampson Low, Marston & Co., Ltd. For the complete listing of the books that are published by Yesterday's Classics, please visit www.yesterdaysclassics. com. Yesterday's Classics is the publishing arm of the Baldwin Online Children's Literature Project which presents the complete text of hundreds of classic books for children at www.mainlesson.com.

ISBN: 978-1-59915-496-1

Yesterday's Classics, LLC
PO Box 339
Ithaca, NY 14851

CONTENTS

GENERAL INTRODUCTION

I

This series of books is intended for two classes of teachers:

1. *For Teachers in Week Day and Sunday Schools.* For these each book is divided into complete lessons. The lesson will demand preparation. Where feasible there should be diligent use of commentaries and of any books indicated in the notes. *As a general rule* I think the teacher should not bring the book at all to his class if he is capable of doing without it. He should make copious notes of the subject. The lesson should be thoroughly studied and digested beforehand, with all the additional aids at his disposal, and it should come forth at the class warm and fresh from his own heart and brain. But I would lay down no rigid rule about the use of the Lesson Book. To some it may be a burden to keep the details of a long lesson in the memory; and, provided the subject has been very carefully studied, the Lesson Book, with its salient points carefully marked in coloured pencil, may be a considerable help. Let each do what seems best in his particular case, only taking care to satisfy his conscience that it is not done through

laziness, and that he can really do best for his class by the plan which he adopts.

2. *For Parents* who would use it in teaching their children at home. They need only small portions, brief little lessons of about ten minutes each night. For these each chapter is divided into short sections. I should advise that on the first night only the Scripture indicated should be read, with some passing remarks and questions to give a grip of the story. That is enough. Then night after night go on with the teaching, taking as much or as little as one sees fit.

I have not written out the teaching in full as a series of readings which could be read over to the child without effort or thought. With this book in hand a very little preparation and adaptation will enable one to make the lesson more interesting and more personal and to hold the child's attention by questioning. Try to get his interest. Try to make him talk. Make the lesson conversational. Don't preach.

II

HINTS FOR TEACHING

An ancient Roman orator once laid down for his pupils the three-fold aim of a teacher:

1. *Placere* (to interest).

2. *Docere* (to teach).

3. *Movere* (to move).

1. To interest the audience (in order to teach them).

2. To teach them (in order to move them).

3. To move them to action.

On these three words of his I hang a few suggestions on the teaching of this set of Lessons.

1. Placere (to interest)

I want especially to insist on attention to this rule. Some teachers seem to think that to interest the pupils is a minor matter. It is not a minor matter and the pupils will very soon let you know it. Believe me, it is no waste of time to spend hours during the week in planning to excite their interest to the utmost. Most of the complaints of inattention would cease at once if the teacher would give more study to rousing their interest. After all, there is little use in knowing the facts of your subject, and being anxious about the souls of the pupils, if all the time that you are teaching, these pupils are yawning and taking no interest in what you say. I know some have more aptitude for teaching than others. Yet, after considerable experience of teachers whose lesson was a weariness to the flesh, and of teachers who never lost attention for a moment, I am convinced, on the whole, that the power to interest largely depends on the previous preparation.

Therefore do not content yourself with merely studying the teaching of this series. Read widely and freely. Read not only commentaries, but books that will give local interest and colour—books that will throw valuable sidelights on your sketch.

But more than reading is necessary. You know the meaning of the expression, *"Put yourself in his place."* Practise that in every Bible story, using your imagination, living in the scene, experiencing, as far as you can, every feeling of the actors. To some this is no effort at all. They feel their cheeks flushing and their eyes growing moist as they project themselves involuntarily into the scene before them. But though it be easier to some than to others, it is in some degree possible to all, and the interest of the lesson largely depends on it. I have done my best in these books to help the teacher in this respect. But no man can help another much. Success will depend entirely on the effort to "put yourself in his place."

In reading the Bible chapter corresponding to each lesson, I suggest that the teacher should read part of the chapter, rather than let the pupils tire themselves by "reading round." My experience is that this "reading round" is a fruitful source of listlessness. When his verse is read, the pupil can let his mind wander till his turn comes again, and so he loses all interest. I have tried, with success, varying the monotony. I would let them read the first round of verses in order; then I would make them read out of the regular order, as I called their names; and sometimes, if the lesson were long, I would again and again interrupt by reading a group of verses myself, making remarks as I went on. To lose their interest is fatal.

I have indicated also in the lessons that you should not unnecessarily give information yourself. Try to question it *into* them. If you tell them facts which they have just read, they grow weary. If you ask a question, and then answer it yourself when they miss it, you cannot keep their attention. Send your questions around in every sort of order, or want of order. Try to puzzle them—try to surprise them. Vary the form of the question, if not answered, and always feel it to be a defeat if you ultimately fail in getting the answer you want.

2. Docere (to teach)

You interest the pupil in order that you may *teach.* Therefore teach definitely the Lesson that is set you. Do not be content with interesting him. Do not be content either with drawing spiritual teaching. Teach the facts before you. Be sure that God has inspired the narration of them for some good purpose.

When you are dealing with Old Testament characters, do not try to shirk or to condone evil in them. They were not faultless saints. They were men like ourselves, whom God was helping and bearing with, as He helps and bears with us, and the interest of the story largely depends on the pupil realizing this.

In the Old Testament books of this series you will find very full chapters written on the Creation, the Fall, the Flood, the election of Jacob, the Sun standing still, the slaughter of Canaanites, and other such subjects. In connection with these I want to say something that especially concerns teachers. Your pupils, now or later, can hardly avoid coming in contact with the flippant scepticism so common nowadays, which makes jests at the story of the sun standing still, and talks of the folly of believing that all humanity was condemned because Eve ate an apple thousands of years ago. This flippant tone is "in the air." They will meet with it in their companions, in the novels of the day, in popular magazine articles on their tables at home. You have, many of you, met with it yourselves; you know how disturbing it is; and you probably know, too, that much of its influence on people arises from the narrow and unwise teaching of the Bible in their youth. Now you have no right to ignore this in your teaching of the Bible. You need not talk of Bible difficulties and their answers. You need not refer to them at all. But teach the truth that will take the sting out of these difficulties when presented in after-life.

To do this requires trouble and thought. We have learned much in the last fifty years that has thrown new light for us on the meaning of some parts of the Bible; which has, at any rate, made doubtful some of our old interpretations of it. We must not ignore this. There are certain traditional theories which some of us still insist on teaching as God's infallible truth, whereas they are really only human opinions about it, which may possibly be mistaken. As long as they are taught as human opinions, even if we are wrong, the mistake will do no harm. But if things are taught as God's infallible truth, to be believed on peril of doubting God's Word, it may do grave mischief, if in after-life the pupil find them seriously disputed, or perhaps false. A shallow, unthinking man, finding part of his teaching false, which has been associated in his mind with the most solemn sanctions of religion, is in danger of letting the whole go. Thus many of our young people drift into hazy doubt about the Bible. Then we get troubled about their beliefs, and give them books of Christian evidences to win them back by explaining that what was taught them in childhood was not *quite* correct, and needs now to be modified by a broader and slightly different view. But we go on as before with the younger generation, and expose them in their turn to the same difficulties.

Does it not strike you that, instead of this continual planning to win men back from unbelief, it might be worth while to try the other method of not exposing them to unbelief? Give them the more careful and intelligent teaching at first, and so prepare them to meet the difficulties by-and-by.

I have no wish to advocate any so-called "advanced" teaching. Much of such teaching I gravely object to. But there are truths of which there is no question amongst thoughtful people, which somehow are very seldom taught to the young, though ignorance about them in after-life leads to grave doubt and misunderstanding. Take, for example, the gradual, progressive nature of God's teaching in Scripture, which makes the Old Testament teaching as a whole lower than that of the New. This is certainly no doubtful question, and the knowledge of it is necessary for an intelligent study of

Scripture. I have dealt with it where necessary in some of the books of this series.

I think, too, our teaching on what may seem to us doubtful questions should be more fearless and candid. If there are two different views each held by able and devout men, do not teach your own as the infallibly true one, and ignore or condemn the other. For example, do not insist that the order of creation must be accurately given in the first chapter of Genesis. You may think so; but many great scholars, with as deep a reverence for the Bible as you have, think that inspired writers were circumscribed by the science of their time. Do not be too positive that the story of the Fall *must be* an exactly literal narrative of facts. If you believe that it is I suppose you must tell your pupil so. But do not be afraid to tell him also that there are good and holy and scholarly men who think of it as a great old-world allegory, like the parable of the Prodigal Son, to teach in easy popular form profound lessons about sin. Endeavor in your Bible teaching "to be thoroughly truthful: to assert nothing as certain which is not certain, nothing as probable which is not probable, and nothing as more probable than it is." Let the pupil see that there are some things that we cannot be quite sure about, and let him gather insensibly from your teaching the conviction that truth, above all things, is to be loved and sought, and that religion has never anything to fear from discovering the truth. If we could but get this healthy, manly, common-sense attitude adopted now in teaching the Bible to young people, we should, with

God's blessing, have in the new generation a stronger and more intelligent faith.

3. *Movere (to move)*

All your teaching is useless unless it have this object: to move the heart, to rouse the affections toward the love of God, and the will toward the effort after the blessed life. You interest in order to teach. You teach in order to move. *That* is the supreme object. Here the teacher must be left largely to his own resources. One suggestion I offer: don't preach. At any rate, don't preach much lest you lose grip of your pupils. You have their attention all right while their minds are occupied by a carefully prepared lesson; but wait till you close your Bible, and, assuming a long face, begin, "And now, boys," etc. and straightway they know what is coming, and you have lost them in a moment.

Do not change your tone at the application of your lesson. Try to keep the teaching still conversational. Try still in this more spiritual part of your teaching to question into them what you want them to learn. Appeal to the judgment and to the conscience. I can scarce give a better example than that of our Lord in teaching the parable of the Good Samaritan. He first interested His pupil by putting His lesson in an attractive form, and then He did not append to it a long, tedious moral. He simply asked the man before Him, "Which of these three *thinkest thou?*"—i.e., "What do you think about it?" The interest was still kept up. The man, pleased at the appeal to his judgment, replied promptly, "He that showed mercy on him;" and on the instant came the quick rejoinder, "Go, and do thou likewise." Thus the lesson ends. Try to work on that model.

Now, while forbidding preaching to your pupils, may I be permitted a little preaching myself? This series of lessons is intended for Sunday schools as well as week-day schools. It is of Sunday-school teachers I am thinking in what I am now about to say. I cannot escape the solemn feeling of the responsibility of every teacher for the children in his care. Some of these children have little or no religious influence exerted on them for the whole week except in this one hour with you. Do not make light of this work. Do not get to think, with good-natured optimism, that all the nice, pleasant children in your class are pretty sure to be Christ's soldiers and servants by-and-by. Alas! for the crowds of these nice, pleasant children, who, in later life, wander away from Christ into the ranks of evil. Do not take this danger lightly. Be anxious; be prayerful; be terribly in earnest, that the one hour in the week given you to use be wisely and faithfully used.

But, on the other hand, be very hopeful too, because of the love of God. He will not judge you hardly. Remember that He will bless very feeble work, if it be your best. Remember that He cares infinitely more for the children's welfare than you do, and, therefore, by His grace, much of the teaching about which you are despondent may bring forth good fruit in the days to come. Do you know the lines about "The Noisy Seven"?—

"I wonder if he remembers—
    Our sainted teacher in heaven—
The class in the old grey schoolhouse,
    Known as the 'Noisy Seven'?

"I wonder if he remembers
    How restless we used to be.
Or thinks we forget the lesson
    Of Christ and Gethsemane?

"I wish I could tell the story
    As he used to tell it then;
I'm sure that, with Heaven's blessing,
    It would reach the hearts of men.

"I often wish I could tell him,
    Though we caused him so much pain
By our thoughtless, boyish frolic,
    His lessons were not in vain.

"I'd like to tell him how Willie,
    The merriest of us all,
From the field of Balaclava
    Went home at the Master's call.

"I'd like to tell him how Ronald,
    So brimming with mirth and fun,
Now tells the heathen of India
    The tale of the Crucified One.

"I'd like to tell him how Robert,
    And Jamie, and George, and 'Ray,'
Are honoured in the Church of God—
    The foremost men of their day.

"I'd like, yes, I'd like to tell him
    What his lesson did for me;
And how I am trying to follow
    The Christ of Gethsemane.

"Perhaps he knows it already,
    For Willie has told him, maybe,
That we are all coming, coming
    Through Christ of Gethsemane.

"How many besides I know not
    Will gather at last in heaven,
The fruit of that faithful sowing,
    But the sheaves are already seven."

LESSON I

THE FIELD OF ZOAN

Read Exodus I.

§ 1. Recapitulation

This story of Exodus is but a continuation of the story we read in Genesis. You remember what we learned there:—

(1) That God had a great purpose for the children of Israel, not for their own sakes, but for the sake of the world, that they should bear the torch of God's light for all the nations upon earth.

(2) That it seems to have been necessary for His purpose that they should go down to live and learn, and suffer in Egypt, and thus become welded into a nation. So God revealed to Abraham what should happen in Egypt, and that afterwards the nation should be restored to Palestine (Genesis xv. 13).

(3) That in His providence, in what seemed the merest chance ways, Joseph got sold into Egypt, and the famine came and drove down his brethren, and he

became prime minister to Pharaoh, and invited down all his family. So God's purpose began to be fulfilled.

(4) That the patriarchs looked forward to the final fulfilment of these promises. Did Abraham see the promises fulfilled? Did Isaac? Did Jacob? What is said in the Epistle to the Hebrews? (xi. 13). "These all died in faith, not having received the promises, but, etc." And then at last Joseph died, with less apparent likelihood of fulfilment than ever. But as he was dying, he took an oath of his brethren, "God will surely visit you, and bring you to the land which He promised, and ye shall carry up my bones from hence." So he died, "and they embalmed him, and he was put in a mummy case in Egypt." (Genesis l. 26). That is the last word of Genesis, and for centuries afterwards careless people in Egypt or Goshen might smile at the foolishness of Joseph's faith. But 500 years later comes Exodus, and then Joshua and the Kings and the Prophets, and at last the coming of Christ, and the long history of the Church. Does it look now as if God had failed in His promise?

§ 2. *The Gap in the Story*

"Joseph died and they put him in a mummy case in Egypt." After this there is a great gap in the story—300 years of silence while the Israelites lived and were enslaved in Egypt, and the mummy of their dead chief lay in its burial case waiting to be carried away when the Deliverance should come. During that long period many stirring events happened in Egypt, changes of dynasties, new races of kings, just as happened in

England when Saxon and Norman and Plantagenet and Tudor dynasties succeeded one after the other to the throne. We know a good deal now about Egyptian history from the many discoveries of monuments of the Pharaohs, and from the writings and pictures that have been found in the old tombs. But they tell us very little about the shepherds from Palestine who had been left in Goshen after the death of the great prime minister Zapenath-Paneah. Enough, however, is known to make the chief students of Egyptian history pretty well agreed as to the period when the Exodus story comes in. More than 2000 years before Christ, they tell us, a great defeat fell upon Egypt. A foreign race, the Hyksos, or Shepherd Kings, invaded the land and subdued it, and reigned as conquerors just as William the Conqueror and his Normans did in the old Saxon days in England. It is thought that one of these Hyksos kings, Apepi, was the Pharaoh of Joseph's day. Then came the Great Revolution, when the native Egyptians rose against them, laid in ruins their royal city of Tanis, and swept them with terrible slaughter from the land, and a native race of kings succeeded to the throne. Then came another revolution, and another new line of Pharaohs, the Rameses dynasty, and it is with the first four of these Rameses kings that our story is concerned. They were called—

Rameses I.

Seti I.

RAMESES II.

MERENPTAH.

This, it is believed, was the new race of kings "that knew not Joseph." In England, when the Normans came, they neither knew nor cared about the great men or the great deeds of the Saxon time. So it would naturally be here. Probably the enslaving of the Israelites began under the first two of these Rameses Pharaohs. Then came the specially cruel treatment under Rameses II., "Rameses the Great," "the Pharaoh of the Oppression." He is known in Egyptian history as the great builder of cities, just the man that would need slaves to work hard for him in the brick-fields. The name of the store city RAMESES seems also to point to him as its builder, since he was the most famous king of that name. And later on some years ago M. Naville discovered and excavated the other store city of Pithom, and found from the inscriptions that King Rameses had been active there. So we have good reason to believe that this great royal builder Rameses II. was really the Pharaoh who oppressed Israel. When he died (Exodus ii. 23) he was succeeded by his son Merenptah, a weaker king, but also a builder, who carried on and completed his father's designs. He, it is believed, was the Pharaoh who contended so fiercely with Moses, and would not let Israel go. Some day you may be able to study for yourselves the reasons which have led Egyptian scholars to fix thus the time of the Exodus. We cannot go into the matter more fully here.

§ 3. The Field of Zoan

Before we begin the story of Moses, would it not be well to have some idea of the place and the times in which its scenes occurred? In the after-life of Israel a place called ZOAN seems to have stood out prominently in the national memory. When speaking of Hebron, the historian says, "it was built seven years before Zoan in Egypt." (Numbers xiii. 22). And when the Psalmist long afterwards is celebrating God's wonders in Egypt, he writes,—

> "Marvellous things did He in the sight of their fathers,
> In the land of Egypt, in the field of Zoan."

And again:—

> "How He had wrought His signs in Egypt,
> And His wonders in the field of Zoan."
> —(Psalm lxxviii. 12, 43)

So if we could find out what and where Zoan was we should probably find out from Egyptian history something more than we are told in the Bible about the story of Israel.

Now we know very well where Zoan is. There is a famous city in ancient history, the city of Tanis or Tsan, the royal city of the shepherd kings, and probably the scene of Joseph's glory, which there are several reasons for identifying with Zoan. One convincing reason is that 700 years after Moses a set of Greek scholars in *Egypt* made the famous Greek translation of the Old Testament known as the Septuagint Bible, and when translating the above verses of the 78th Psalm they rendered it,—

17

"Marvellous things did He in the sight of their fathers,
In the land of Egypt, in the field of Tanis."

Therefore they, residing in Egypt at a time when Tanis was still a flourishing provincial town, must have known that Zoan was but another name for the once famous Tanis, which had been the royal city of the Pharaohs in the land of Goshen 700 years before.

Egyptian history is perfectly clear as to the fact that Zoan or Tanis, which had been destroyed in the Great Revolution, when the Hyksos were driven out with great slaughter, was afterwards rebuilt in glory and splendour by Rameses the Great, "the Pharaoh of the Oppression." It was his royal city, and therefore, if scholars are right in fixing the date of the Exodus, Tanis would be certainly the city of Moses, and if we could form any idea of its appearance in the days of its glory, we should be able to call up in our minds in some degree some of the greatest scenes of his life.

§ 4. *The Grave of a Dead City*

Far away in the Delta of the Nile, in the centre of the ancient land of Goshen there lies to-day, the grave of a dead city. It is like a great sand island heaped up into desolate piles of reddish brown mud and strewed all over with ruins. Nearly forty years ago (in 1884) a boat arrived one morning at the side of this desolate mound, and a traveller sprang ashore to view the dreary ruins in the dim light of the morning. The mound covered the ruins of the ancient city of Zoan, or Tanis, and the traveller was the famous explorer, Dr. Flinders Petrie, sent out from England by the Egypt Exploration Fund, to uncover this lost city of the Pharaohs. Some time before they had sent out a Frenchman, M. Naville, for the purpose, but he thought the task too great for the time at his disposal, and, turning aside in another direction, came unexpectedly upon the most fortunate find of his life, the buried store city of Pithom,[1] which the Israelites had built for Pharaoh (Exodus i. 11).

So the exploring of Tanis remained for an Englishman. For five months Dr. Petrie worked at the ruins with his little band of helpers. He dug and explored and measured and photographed, till he had found and given to the world a list of the buried wonders, and an idea of what the ancient Tanis was like.[2]

Digging for Egyptian cities is a curious sort of work, for usually there are two or three of them one under the other. Hundreds of years before Moses there was the older city of Tanis, the great royal city of the Hyksos Shepherd Kings, and probably the scene of Joseph's glory. In the Great Revolution that I told you of, this ancient Tanis was laid in utter ruins, and probably remained so for centuries getting gradually covered by the drifting desert sands. Then after centuries came King Rameses II., the Pharaoh of the Oppression, and rebuilt it in great stateliness and grandeur. And ages later

[1] See *The Store City of Pithom* by E. Naville, published by the Egypt Exploration Fund.

[2] See *Tanis* by Flinders Petrie (Trübner & Co.).

still, there was a Roman town there, whose people were walking about over the buried statues and buildings of King Rameses' day. And even in Christian days it became the seat of a Christian bishopric, probably on account of the persistent Coptic tradition that it was the city of Moses' birth. So you see Dr. Petrie had no easy task when he gathered his crowd of Arab labourers to dig up the buried city of Moses and King Rameses.

First he found the ruins of a long double row of pillars and sphinxes, which he saw at once must have been the avenue of the temple. So he set to work and exposed the pillars and statues and the sphinxes of black marble, with their strange human faces and lion bodies. Then he dug on to the red granite temple, 1000 feet long, and the old houses of the city. But he could not get very far on with the work. "We can only imagine," he says, "what interest may await us when we reach the dwellings of the people who lived around the splendid temple . . . replete with noble statues, and dominated in every part by the royal splendour of RAMESES beloved by Amon."[1] There could certainly be no question as to King Rameses' connection with it. Everywhere was the name of this vainglorious Pharaoh. Not content with his

---

[1] And still more so surely when they dig down lower still where, he says, "must lie the older town, the town of the bearded Hyksos." He got some of their statues there, "all distinguished by an entirely different type of face to any in other Egyptian monuments, and which cannot be attributed to any other known period. It is therefore all the more certain that they belong to this foreign race." Also they are without exception of the black or grey granite, never of the favourite red granite. The Hyksos had no control of the red granite quarries of Assuan, so had to use black.

own pillars and sphinxes, Dr. Petrie found that he had chiselled off the names of the more ancient kings from their monuments, and everywhere covered them with his own. All the ruins told of King Rameses, how he had rebuilt Zoan and adorned it with splendid statues and buildings. The temple was so full of his monuments and inscriptions that one might almost believe that he himself was the god who was worshipped there. And what an old boaster he was! He calls himself "the Smiter of Nations, the Strong Bull, the Destroyer of His Enemies, Rames beloved of (the god) Amon." (See Flinders Petrie, *Tanis*.)

Though Dr. Petrie found these splendid memorials overthrown and displaced, yet one could well imagine them whole and erect—one could imagine the scene in those far back days, when King Rameses reigned and worshipped in the temple, walking in procession through his grand avenue of sphinxes and obelisks, to worship the Sun and the River as gods, to be worshipped himself almost as a god. We cannot yet identify where his palace and public buildings stood, but we can see where he had erected, overtopping the city, the most stupendous monument that ever man had raised to himself, a great colossal statue, carved out of one solid block of red granite, 90 feet high, and weighing over 900 tons! Think of the vast labour and probably the cruel slave-driving involved in cutting that giant block from its far-off quarry, and bearing it to its destination right across Egypt. One can see the huge brick wall of the city crumbled into dust, and one can guess that somewhere, amid all its grandeur, there were rows of mean little slave huts, somewhere along the river, where men and women lived like beasts of burden, in pain and degradation, thinking that neither God nor man cared anything about them.

If we had sufficient money and leisure would it not be interesting to start off all of us together by the morning train to the ruins of Tanis to study on the spot the childhood of Moses? It would take us some weeks to go, and we must carry plenty of provisions, for Dr. Petrie found it very hard to get anything to eat. Fancy our sitting down next month on a piece of that huge statue of King Rameses, and thinking of the time when it was such a familiar object to the eyes of Moses, and when the Israelite slaves used to look up to it across the river and curse it and the tyrant in their bitter hearts! Then we might turn and look eastward for the Exodus route. Aye, we might go back 500 years earlier still, and think of the older city underneath the city of Rameses, and watch in imagination the splendid funeral of Jacob as it started from Tanis away to the far-off grave of his fathers in Hebron. *From Zoan to Hebron!* I think I should like to open my Bible just then and read with a new connection that verse I have referred to (Numbers xiii. 22): "Now Hebron was built seven years before Zoan in Egypt."

§ 5. How Pharaoh "Dealt Wisely"

Now we are ready to read our lesson for to-day (Exodus i.). We can imagine the Pharaoh in his splendid new city of Tanis, with its stately buildings and its avenue

22

of obelisks and sphinxes leading to the great temple, and his huge red statue, 90 feet high, commanding the whole scene. And outside, the bands of slaves bending under the whip of the taskmasters, and cursing Pharaoh and his vanity and cruelty, and the clever statesmanship that had "dealt wisely" with them, so as to gradually break down their spirit till they were too cowed and degraded to rise in the might of their numbers against him.

Pharaoh was afraid that their numbers would make them dangerous in case of a war—but he was also afraid that they should "get them up out of the land" (v. 10), and that he should lose all this valuable slave labour, so much wanted for his great buildings and for digging canals, and working at the hardest task in Egypt, the artificial watering of the land that was out of reach of the river. (See v. 14, for the two sorts of work.) So King Rameses "dealt wisely" with them, and got his fears quieted, and his lands watered, and his two store cities of Pithom and Rameses built. That was all that concerned him. Never mind Right or Mercy. Never mind Justice and the God of Justice if he can get his own will done.

But somehow Justice and the God of Justice are not so easily flung aside. No king or nation can do these things without putting themselves wrong with God, whether it be in Egypt long ago, or in America to-day. So God had to punish Egypt and to deliver Israel. Not that He was against Egypt any more than against Israel. This is no story of God's favouritism for one people as against another. It is the lesson of a divine eternal law that must be always and everywhere against wrong.

People don't think that God is watching—I am sure Pharaoh did not. And I am pretty sure the Israelites did not as they struggled on in their hopeless misery. I dare say they often thought with bitter mockery of the dead Joseph in his lonely mummy case, and of his hopeful prophecy, that God would surely visit them and deliver them. Yet all the time God's plan was being silently and slowly worked out, as we shall see in the following chapters.

NOTES

Exodus xii. 41 gives the Israelites' sojourn as 430 years. The genealogies and the Egyptian chronology tend to confirm this. Rawlinson's *Moses* conjecturally divides the period thus:—70 years under Joseph's protection, 160 years in which they were "afflicted," but not severely oppressed, and 100 years in which "their lives were made bitter, and the Egyptians made them to serve with rigour." (Exodus i. 14).

Probably the extreme measure of destroying the male infants was a temporary one, owing to dread of the formidable Kheta or Hittite race. They were a frequent source of uneasiness to Egypt, and the Israelites occupied the frontier which would first be attacked in an invasion by them. Naturally Pharaoh feared that they would side with the invaders, and so win their freedom, and all the more so since they probably resembled them in language, costume, habits, etc.

Verse 11, "Treasure Cities."—The Hebrew word corresponds very closely both in form and meaning with "magazines," depots of ammunition and provisions; the same word is used in 1 Kings ix. 19; 2 Chronicles viii. 4, and xxxii. 28.

Captives were employed in great numbers for building and enlarging such depots under the Egyptian kings of the 18th and 19th dynasties.—*Speaker's Commentary.*

QUESTIONS FOR LESSON I

Who is the chief person in the Exodus story?

Who was chief person dealt with at the end of Genesis?

What did Joseph prophesy as he died?

How many years had passed before the Exodus began?

Who was King Rameses?

Can you tell anything of the discovery of Moses' old city?

What was the condition of the Israelites in Egypt in Moses' day?

LESSON II

THE TRAINING OF
THE DELIVERER

Read Exodus II. 1-10.

Acts VII. 17-22.

§ 1. Moses' Infancy

Do you remember in *Uncle Tom's Cabin* the little slave hut of Uncle Tom and Aunt Chloe, with their merry little boys Mose and Pete? I am thinking now of a slave hut like it out by the brick-fields of Tanis 3000 years ago, where another godly slave man and his wife tried to bring up their children in the fear of the Lord. What were their names? Of what tribe? (Daughter=descendant, no reason for the common notion that Jochebed was elderly and was Amram's aunt.) Perhaps in more prosperous days they belonged to high family in the tribe, but now all was changed. I can fancy this poor slave father working naked in the hot brick-fields or at the canal, and coming home at night weary and bleeding from the overseer's whip, and perhaps for the moment inclined to doubt in his sore heart if God saw or cared at all.

Why should we think it was a religious home? Were all the Israelites in Egypt religious? No (Joshua xxiv. 14; Ezekiel xx. 5-9). But here, when we see all God's providential care afterwards for the bringing up and training of the Deliverer, we can hardly doubt he would be born into a religious home. And also in the New Testament we hear of the faith of his parents (Hebrews xi. 23). What other children? Miriam, the first Mary in the Bible, about fifteen, and a little boy Aaron, three years old (*ch.* vii. 7), able to run about and delight his mother with his funny baby talk. I wonder how he escaped being thrown into the river? Probably because he was born before this cruel order, and that it applied only to babies.

Now into this home, with the cruel order hanging over the people, a little boy was born. Was he ugly? (see *ch.* ii. 2; Acts vii. 20; Hebrews xi. 23). I dare say his mother would have thought him lovely in any case. They always do. But this baby was especially so, and his mother was all the more drawn to him. Generally great joy about a new baby. Was it so here? Why not? Oh, what an awful dread they had of the king's inspectors, and the dark river, and the horrible crocodiles waiting for their prey! What did Jochebed do? Hid the baby. Children warned not to tell. How long hidden? A baby three months old with healthy lungs is not easy to hide. So the poor distracted mother had to find some other plan. Do you think she prayed and trusted God about it? (Hebrews xi. 23).

What was her plan? Yes; we are told by Josephus, the Jewish historian,[1] that Pharaoh's daughter, the Princess Thermuthis, was married and childless, and greatly longed for a child. If it was so, the quick-witted mother would know it. At any rate it was her only chance. And so we can picture her in the early dawn stealing along with her baby, terrified lest he should cry and betray her, till she got to the reeds in the secluded water where the princess went down to bathe. We can see her placing the little ark in the reeds and passionately kissing her little boy and lifting her streaming eyes to Heaven as she commends him to God's care. We know exactly what such a mother would do. Then the wise little sister was set to watch.

Now tell me what happened? How did she guess it was a Hebrew child? Perhaps the features and dress and the knowledge that only a Hebrew mother would risk her baby's life like this. See the simple way, like mere chance, in which God answered the poor mother's prayers. The princess was childless, and the baby was very beautiful, and when he looked at her and cried in his helplessness and fright, her heart went out at once to the little crying child. I think Moses, who tells the story, likes to dwell on her kindness and compassion. I daresay he loved her a good deal, and that she was dead when he wrote the story, and he liked to think of her kindly heart. People who are not accustomed to thinking of God in human affairs would call these things chance. Do you think so? Do you not think the

---

[1] *Antiquities of the Jews*, II. 9, §4, 5.

parents' prayers and faith and God's high purpose for
the child had something to do with it?

Tell me now of Miriam's clever little plan. Do you
think the princess suspected it? I should not wonder if
she did, especially when she saw how the mother held
and looked at her child. But if the princess suspected
she held her tongue about it, and sent the child away
to be nursed for her. I suppose she would not dare to
take it to the palace. How glad that little mother was
that night as she carried home her baby safe and secure,
and how her faith would be strengthened, and how she
and her husband and children would bow down before
God in thankfulness for His answer to their prayers.

§ 2. His Boyhood, His Mother's Bible

So during his early years the boy remained at home
with his mother. How would this affect God's plan for
his future? Don't you see? The early years of a child are
the most important time with regard to his religion.
The teaching and the feelings about God and the habit
of prayer and trust acquired in our childhood sink
more deeply into us than any later teaching. We can
remember best of all the hymns and prayers learnt in
our childhood. So you see, instead of the child being
taught to worship the sacred hawk and the black bull in
the big red temple of Pharaoh, he was here in his earliest
years in the hands of a mother who loved and trusted
God, and who would teach him to love and worship
God as she did herself. That was the grand foundation
for the religion of his after life.

Did you ever wonder what Bible Moses' mother had, and how did he and Joseph and the ancient Israelites learn about God? As far as we can learn there existed, long before a word of Genesis was written, a sort of "Bible before the Bible." There was the Creation Story, The Story of the Fall, The Story of the Flood, etc. Perhaps they were written down before Abraham's day, when writing was well known. More probably they were handed down from father to son, and preserved in memory in the folk lore of the people without any writing. So Moses may well have learned them from his mother in the slave hut. (See my Introduction to Genesis in this series.)

Of course, as the child grew up he had to leave his mother and go to live in the palace to play with princely companions, and be waited on by courtly attendants, and be surrounded by all the refinement and luxury of the most refined and luxurious court in the world. There would doubtless be much of servile flattery and obedience to his every whim. There is always much in the position of a young prince to spoil his nature, whether in Egypt or anywhere else. And I fear in Egypt Moses would see much that was not good for a boy to see. Don't you think it was a good thing for him that he had been brought up by a religious mother? Ah! that is about the best thing God can give to any of us.

As I look at Dr. Petrie's photographs of what he found in the buried city where Moses had lived, and still more as I see the strange old pictures of Egyptian life that have come down to us from the time of Moses, I can picture the sights around the boy as he looked from the palace roof, or drove in his little chariot through the city, the streets swarming with gaily-dressed crowds, the river crowded with barges in full sail, the music and song, the procession of priests down that long avenue of sphinxes to the great temple of Ptah; and sometimes, on more exciting days, the return of the king from some triumphant expedition with his kilted soldiers and bright swift chariots, and the long rows of captives dragged through the streets. Wonderful sights in that ancient city of Tanis, where Moses was a boy, with the grey mysterious desert stretching away behind, a wonderful delightful life for a boy, flattered and petted and admired like this young prince Moses. I wonder if he ever saw the darker side of that life—the hot brick-fields in the blazing sun, and the slaves sweating at their tasks and crying out under the cruel lash. I wonder too if the little mother who so loved him and prayed for him was ever allowed to see him in his palace days, or was the new royal mother so jealous of his love that she shut out the poor parents from him altogether? Did the poor mother die without her child beside her? Was Amram flogged to death in the brick-fields before the boy grew up? And had they to wait till they passed into the Waiting Life beyond the grave to understand God's high plans for their son in the palace? I should not wonder if it were so.

§ 3. His Education, His Copybook

One thing at any rate was well attended to in King Rameses' days—the education of boys of high rank.

In his boyhood Moses would be taught reading and writing, but not so simply as they are taught in our country to-day. His books were like rows of curious pictures. When he was learning to read the old writings and the inscriptions and monuments he found that an eagle meant *a*, and an owl was *m*, a chicken was *u*, a hawk stood for *hur*, and a vulture for *mut*. But when he had to write them in his copybook he found that the pictures had to change their forms a good deal for the convenience of rapid writing. Should you like to see one of Moses' copybooks? I cannot show you that, but I can show you one like it. Here is the reproduction from a photograph of one.

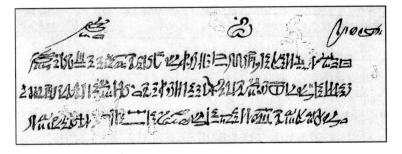

WHAT MOSES' COPYBOOK WAS LIKE

Photograph of an Egyptian boy's copybook about the time of Moses (*Anastasian Papyri*, 5, 16). The left-hand word of the first line, *asha* (="much") is corrected as not written well enough. From Erman's *Ancient Egypt*.

It was not written by Moses, but by another Egyptian boy of about the same period or a little earlier. There are several of them in the museums, for when a boy of high rank died, his copybooks, the only achievement of his youthful powers, were frequently buried with him. An Egyptian copybook is easily recognized from its size and shape and often from the writing-master's corrections over the line. In this photograph you can see how at one end of the first line the boy had written badly the word 'asha' which means *much*, and how the teacher had corrected it just above. I can even tell you how many pages of copybook one Egyptian boy had to do each day. For one copybook is dated on one page the 24th of the month Epiphi, and three pages back is the 23rd, and three pages forward the 25th Epiphi. So that boy had to write three pages a day.[1]

I think boys were pretty much the same in Moses' time as they are to-day. I notice that at the back of the copybooks are all sorts of scribbling and queer boyish pictures of houses and cows and drawings of men in that sort of high art which belongs to idle schoolboys from time immemorial, with round head and dots for the eyes and hands sticking out like garden rakes. Only I think the idle boys in Moses' day got a little more flogging than such boys do now. For here are some of the schoolmasters' opinions and advice. "The youth has a back he attends when it is beaten." "Spend no day in idleness or thou wilt be flogged; for the ears of a boy are placed on his back and he hears when it is flogged."[2] And so one is not surprised to read that "at noon the children rushed out of school *shouting for joy!*" I dare say Moses was much the same sort of boy as yourselves, only I don't think he was idle, else he could hardly have been so "learned in all the wisdom of

[1] See Erman's *Life in Ancient Egypt*, ch. xiv.

[2] Anastasi Papyri 5, 8, 6 in British Museum quoted in Erman's *Ancient Egypt*.

the Egyptians." Besides, reading and writing he would learn also arithmetic and music, and what probably he liked better, games of wrestling and fencing, games of draughts, and the various games of ball depicted in Egyptian paintings.

§ 4. His Youth and Manhood

And when he grew up he was of course sent to one of the two great ancient universities—the Oxford and Cambridge or the Harvard and Yale of Egypt. Tradition says that On or Heliopolis was his college city. You remember it was there that Joseph met his wife, "Asenath, daughter of Potipherah, priest of On." (Genesis xli. 45). Here in this college they taught all the higher branches of learning. They taught chiefly religion as it was understood in Egypt—a wonderful religion, with its popular side for the common crowd, its sacred hawks, and bulls, and crocodiles to be worshipped—and yet behind all that, the belief in one God great and good, who was behind and above all these, and who demanded that men should be righteous and true. They had a wonderful book, the "Book of the Dead," which surely must have been an inspiration from God, telling of a future life and the Judgment of the Soul. It helps us to understand that the Spirit of God was not confined to the Jews only; that in all the nations of the earth God left not Himself without witness in some degree. Besides religion, they taught Astronomy, Law, and Medicine, and Literature, and the art of writing poetry, which Moses made such good use of in after days (Exodus xv., Deuteronomy xxxii.).

Do you think he attended to his studies? See what St. Stephen says (Acts vii. 22), "learned in all the wisdom of the Egyptians." And what else?—"and mighty in word and in deed." In his days, as in our own, the only way in which a prince could be mighty in deeds was by joining the army. It is what we should expect of a prince of Egypt. The Pharaohs were great warriors and led their own soldiers in person. We have several pictures of this king Rameses of Moses' day at the head of his army, and accordingly Jewish tradition tells us that Moses was a soldier, that he became a great warrior and led an expedition against the Ethiopians, from which he came back in triumph. Probably he served too in the Hittite wars of King Seti and King Rameses, and all this experience would be most useful in later days when he had to marshal the great Israelite host. Again you see God's hand preparing him for his future. His study of Law and his knowledge of literature helped him to legislate for Israel. His acquaintance with the Egyptian religion helped him in his appeals to Pharaoh's conscience. His experience of war made him a fit leader of men. In his boyish lessons and his college studies and his drill in the Egyptian barracks, he probably had no idea that he was preparing himself for the future which God had before him; yet because he did them well he was more useful. So with our boys too. They have their lessons to learn and their work to do, and their business is just to do their best at them—looking forward to the future and trying to make themselves thoroughly fitted to do useful work for God. But chiefly I want you to see here the wonderful way in which God by ordinary means got his great plans worked out. For He is doing just the same to-day. Next chapter tells of Moses' great life decision.

QUESTIONS FOR LESSON II

Who were (1) Aaron, (2) Miriam, (3) the Princess?

Who was the child born in the slave hut?

What great danger was he in and how was he saved?

God had a plan for Moses' life. How was it helped by (1) being with his mother, (2) by his training in college and in the army?

While he was a young prince in the palace where was his family?

THE GREAT LIFE DECISION

Read Exodus II. 11-16.

Acts VII. 23-34.

Hebrews XI. 24-28.

§ 1. The Decision

Recapitulate—GOD'S providence—Moses preserved—guarded—educated—trained—as a scholar—a
leader—a warrior—unconsciously prepared for God's
high purpose.

We follow on to see the result of all this training. The
next glimpse we get of him is when he is a full-grown
man—in high position, a prince of Egypt, perhaps a
victorious general—with men bowing down to him as he
drove through the streets and crying before his chariot,
"Bow the knee." How old was he? (Acts vii. 23). When he
was full forty years old, what happened? "It came into
his heart, etc." Who put it into his heart? Do you think it
had never before come into his heart? I am pretty sure it
had. But oh! it was very hard to do it. He was but a man

like us, and therefore right doing was often hard and painful. I have often wondered about him before he was forty years old—during his college days at Heliopolis, and his wars and his great military and social success, with all men bowing down before him—what of his old father, the slave Amram, in the brick-fields, and the little mother that had dared and suffered so much for him? What of Aaron and Miriam and all their relatives and friends who were working at the canals and at the store city of Pithom? Had the princess entirely cut off all communication? Did he know nothing of them? Had he forgotten them? Probably the old father and mother were dead. And, if so, was it possible—don't you think it might be possible, or even likely, that the brilliant young captain in the royal palace should be a little ashamed of his slave origin, and seek to hide it? And, if so, don't you think it likely that the God "from whom all holy desires, all good counsels, and all just works do proceed," in His constant discipline of the young man should have often made "it come into his heart" this duty he was shirking—just as He makes us think and feel pain in our conscience? Did you ever feel this when you were trying to escape doing something that you felt you ought to do. *(Try to bring this home to the pupils.)* Marvellous, this constant discipline of God with us all. Never violently breaking down our will, but touching us, and troubling us, and kindly, patiently waiting for us to yield.

As he grew older, I think his conscience hurt him more, and I think, too, the conviction stole on him that God had given him his high position for the sake of his poor brethren (Acts vii. 25). Perhaps his mother had taught him that long ago. Of course we are only guessing about this struggle in Moses' heart. But if we are right, it is interesting to think that he was but a poor struggler after right, like ourselves, and that it was God's grace that helped him to conquer. It was not till he was forty years old that he grew ashamed of his meanness and went out like a true man to visit his poor brethren.

He knew that this meant breaking with all his high courtly life in the palace. Do you think it was easy? For this young captain had no doubt grand prospects before him and the ambition that belongs to genius and to youth, and the keen love of pleasure that young men have. Must he crush it all and take his place with these outcast slaves? Yes, said the voice of duty, the voice of God within him. "You must, or be no true man." And he did it. It took forty years to make him noble enough to do it; but it was done, and so the first great step in God's discipline of him was gained. "By faith he refused to be the son of Pharaoh's daughter, etc." (Hebrews xi. 24.)

"By faith." Some commentators say that Moses' faith meant his belief that the 400 years of God's prophecy to Abraham were nearly accomplished, and that God by his hand would deliver them. Maybe that was true too. But I think Moses' faith meant especially this—the faith of all true men in God's blessing and approval when with an honest and true heart they choose what seems to them the Right.

Remember whenever you have to choose between

the Right and the Pleasant, that there are two sides of your nature engaged—the high noble side, with the Holy Spirit prompting it, and the low, mean side with the Devil behind it; and whenever you yield to the higher side you are following God's leading—God's plan for your life whether you can see it or not. I am sure Moses did not see all that depended on his choice. He did not know when he obeyed his higher impulses that he was unconsciously falling in with God's great plan for Israel. We each have our part too in God's great plan for helping the world, sometimes a very little part, and we cannot know what it will be. But we may be certain in all our struggles and decisions that every choice for the right is a stepping forward on God's life-path for us as surely as if God had given us a written chart of the path. Do you think Moses ever repented this life choice? Do you think you or anybody will ever repent choosing for God and Right?

§ 2. The Result

From Hebrews xi. it seems that the change in Moses' life was not from a mere chance killing of an Egyptian, but from a deliberate decision that he would renounce his palace life to champion the cause of the slaves. I think this renunciation came before he killed the Egyptian. I can imagine his relief when his decision was made; but also, I can imagine his pain at telling the kind princess, who had been as a mother to him, if she were still living. And I can picture the wonder in the palace, in the army, amongst his comrades, the young nobles of Egypt, that any man should be fool enough to make the great renunciation for the sake of a set of outcast slaves. Perhaps some few were noble enough to understand him. Most thought him mad. But whatever they thought, the prince, the warrior, the comrade, went out from among them forever—out from the palace of Pharaoh, perhaps to the slave huts in the brick-fields.

Should not you expect he would have been received with delight and gratitude and applause? Perhaps he expected it. Was he so received? I picture him day by day visiting his brethren on the plains of Tel es Maskouteh, raging in secret at the horrors which he saw. We know from the old writings and from the paintings on the tombs what the flogging of slaves was like. At last it grew beyond bearing. He saw a poor Hebrew being flogged, perhaps to death, in a lonely corner of the brick-fields, and in a moment his blood was up, and in the fierce hot rush of his anger he smote that Egyptian taskmaster dead to the ground. Do you think he was wrong? I do not think God would condemn fierce indignation against cruelty and oppression. Yet, perhaps, he was too hasty and passionate. It looks as if he needed the long training in Midian to teach calmness and self-control before he took on him the leading of that unruly, irritating host of Israel. Probably it deserved both praise and blame. At any rate, surely he thought, my brethren will be on my side. What happened next day when he interfered? Ah, yes; all his sympathy and self-sacrifice only called out their sneers and threats to inform on him. Slavery had so degraded them.

Don't you think it was a sore disappointment to

41

Moses? Do you think God ought to have rewarded his nobleness better? But God's rewards for being good are not mere applause or gain, or glory of men. God rewards a man for being good by making him better still. And sometimes he can only do that by sorrow and pain and disappointment. And so God let this come to him that in his disappointment from men he might cling more to God, who never disappoints.

Perhaps, too, Moses did not yet see his own helplessness and the need of entire dependence on God for himself and for Israel. No doubt he knew that he was clever and capable, and that he had done a splendid thing in making his life decision. That was all true, but perhaps he needed some of the conceit about it taken out of him. I think I should if I had been in his place. He needed more training and refining to fit him for the great task before him. So what happened? Yes; he had to fly from his old friends of Egypt and his poor brethren of Israel, and go away into a lonely exile. He had to live all those years in Midian with a wife who, I think, never understood him. He had to feel even doubtful whether God was pleased with him and whether he had not done more harm than good.

Do you think it was hard? Did he feel it keenly? Would you feel it keenly? Of course he felt it. Look at the bitterness in the name of his first-born son (Exodus xviii. 3, 4), Gershom, "a stranger here." But it was God's blessed training all the time, and I think he began to know it before he named his second boy. What? "My God is a help."

So we must leave Moses to-day going through the hard, lonely, yet blessed training of God. And we learn from to-day's lesson, what? First, that the best thing in the whole world for any man is to choose right, even if he were never rewarded for it here. Second, that when loneliness, and sickness, and sorrow come to people they are not always an evil. This is often God's way of bestowing on them His very best.

QUESTIONS FOR LESSON III

How old was Moses when he thought of visiting his slave people?

Why did he kill the Egyptian slave-driver?

How did this change his whole life?

What do you know of his life in Midian?

Who were (1) Jethro, (2) Gershom, (3) Eliezer?

What do we learn from the names of Moses' sons?

LESSON IV

THE CALL OF MOSES

Read Exodus III. 4-17.

§ 1. Waiting

The scene is changed. Many years have elapsed. Instead of great Tanis, with its crowded streets, its palaces, its temples, and its great red statue of King Rameses, there is a lonely pasture land in the shadow of the mountains, and a quiet, thoughtful, grey-haired man walking over the pastures. What land? What man? Minding sheep instead of leading armies. What a change for Moses!

Does not it seem like a great waste of time that he should lose all those best years of his life in these lonely pastures when so much great work was waiting for him? Was it waste? Why not? God was training him and fitting him for his great future, accustoming him to the desert life in which Israel must live, teaching calmness and self-control, and drawing him nearer to Himself. Do you think Moses had any idea of this purpose of God in his banishment? I don't. I fancy he

44

thought himself a failure and mistaken, and that if Israel was to be helped some one else must do it. He did not know that God was fitting him for his future. Don't you think he had much fitness already? A scholar, a warrior, a leader of men. Don't you think he was a good man already after his grand life decision? Yes, but not good enough. God wanted to make him far better, and truer, and nobler, to take all the pride and self-confidence out of him, and by all those years of thought and prayer and communing with God on the lonely pastures to make him one of the noblest men the world ever saw. If he had known, I think he would have been happier all those years. I think most of us would be happier in our sorrows if we knew that God was watching us and training us by them.

§ 2. The Presence of God

At last he learned the meaning of it all. Think of him on that memorable day of his life, walking up the lonely mountain, puzzling about the strange mystery of life, puzzling, perhaps, about the strong belief of Abraham, and Jacob, and Joseph as to the people's deliverance— wondering, perhaps, if his own rashness had thwarted God's good purposes for them. Ah, it was hard to understand. He could remember how eager he had been, how he had given up his great position for what seemed to him God's will for Israel, and now it seemed all a stupid waste of a life. It seemed all a mistake. It seemed that God did not want him after all.

And then, suddenly, as he was walking and thinking,

a strange thing happened. What did he see? What was so strange about it? While Moses stood wondering what was revealed to him? That he was in God's presence. Did it frighten him? Had he been just as much in God's presence all the time before? What difference? Just that he did not know it. All the time of his babyhood and danger, all the time in the palace, all the time of that long contest in his heart as to whether he would go out from his high position to live among the slaves, God was about him, watching and helping. But just at this moment God withdrew the veil and let Moses know. That seems always the way. Not that God had just come to the place, but—? yes, that He had made His presence felt. Is it so now? I read once an old ghost story, in which the dead man used to come and sit invisible amongst his living friends. What a strange feeling it would give us—an invisible person sitting in this class and sometimes showing signs of his presence. Yet it is so always, in trouble, in temptation, in secret sin, in all life God is near, though he does not withdraw the veil now as He did at times long ago. Should not it make one solemn? and glad when we do good? and frightened when we do evil?

How surprised Moses was that all those forty years God had been near, reading all his thoughts. Had God been near the poor slaves, too, all that time? (read *vv.* 7, 8, 9). How wonderful it would seem to Moses! He thought God had forgotten them and himself, and now he hears God say, what? "I have seen the affliction, I have heard their cry, I know their sorrows, I am come down to deliver them." Oh, what a glad, blessed, wonderful world it would be if people could learn that lesson.

§ 3. *The Call of Moses*

Was Moses right forty years before in thinking that it was God who was prompting him to go and help the poor slaves? Where was he mistaken? I think the fit time was not come. He was not ready and they were not ready, and perhaps the Canaanites in Palestine were not ready yet for being cast out. God wanted to give them every chance (Genesis xv. 16). Whenever any prompting to do an unselfish, noble act comes to us, don't you think we may generally feel sure it is God who is prompting it, as in Moses' case? And to those who obey it continually do you think God reveals Himself as He did to Moses? Not in a burning bush or an angelic vision—but in the strong growing sense of His presence and His love.

What was God's commission to Moses? (*v.* 10). Was he very eager to go? He was no longer the eager young soldier of forty years ago who felt that he could do anything and conquer anybody, as he had conquered the Ethiopians. He had less belief in himself now. Is that bad for a man? Well, I think it generally is. A man who is very timid and diffident is not fit to be a leader. But in Moses' case I think it was good—why? Because, as I learn from his after-life, it prepared him to cast himself fully on God and to trust utterly and entirely in God's strength instead of his own. I don't think he could ever have got through that terrible after-experience in the wilderness but for his strong trust in God.

I think his hesitation was unreasonably excessive, but notice, it was not through any fear of danger, but lest he should injure the cause. What was his first excuse and God's reply? (*vv.* 11, 12). What a grand reply, full of hope and strength for him. All his terrible desert experience afterwards he had to rest on that and it never failed him. Will it fail us? When can we be sure of that promise? Whenever, like Moses, we are on the path of duty. What further encouragement did he get from God's name? His further excuse? (iv. 1). How was this answered? He would feel at once that God's power was behind him when he could do such miracles, and that if with a common rod God could enable him to do such things, God could surely use him, weak and unworthy and unfit as he was. That is the great comfort for every one who sees a plain duty before him. To see a plain duty is like a clear call from God and we must always trust God to see us through with it.

Now tell me Moses' last excuse and how it was answered? (iv. 10).

§ 4. *Preparation for Egypt*

So Moses returned to Jethro's encampment to prepare for his mission.

Do you think Moses would sleep much that night? What exciting thoughts—the old ambition of his youth come back to him—he was to be the leader and deliverer of Israel and he must go away at once on his mission to Pharaoh—and Aaron, the brother whom he had not seen for all these long years, was coming to meet him and be his comrade. But above all else would come one thought overtopping all the rest. What? The revelation that had come into his heart that day—that God was always near.

NOTES

Verse 6. Compare our Lord's reference to this (Mark xii. 26) as a proof of Resurrection, "how in The Bush God spoke," i.e. in the Scripture section called "The Bush."

Verse 15. Point out that the word LORD in capital letters in Old Testament always represents the word Jehovah. Read this—"Jehovah, God of, etc."

Verse 22. *Shall borrow*, a most mischievous translation, which has continually puzzled and disturbed Bible readers. The words mean *ask, demand*, and there is no justification for the translation *borrow*. The Israelites were to *demand* as their right from the Egyptians, as some little remuneration for their long terrible work in Egypt, and the Egyptians in their terror after the death of the first born granted the demand.

Note.—In Rawlinson's *Moses*, an interesting illustration of this history is given by means of an Old Egyptian writing, "The Story of Sanehat." Sanehat wanders from the Egyptian court and reaches Edom. The sheikh receives him, questions him, gives him his daughters in marriage. "Here," he says, "I passed many years, children were born to me, the sheikh was satisfied with me and loved me and made me chief of his children." Still he was always longing for Egypt; and by and by, when the way was open and the sheikh gave his consent, he returns to Pharaoh's court to be numbered among his councillors. The story interestingly exhibits the movements of a refugee from Pharaoh's court and the possibility of return after many years.

QUESTIONS FOR LESSON IV

Had God forgotten the poor slaves all this time?

Tell of God's call to Moses.

What did God tell him about his watching over the slaves?

Does God's call ever come to men now? How?

How did Moses feel about God's command to him?

Tell some of his excuses.

LESSON V

THE RETURN TO EGYPT

Read Exodus IV. 29 to V. 23.

§ 1. *The Condition of the Slaves*

Recapitulate. Forty years in Midian. God's message from the burning bush.

During all these forty years in Midian how had things been going on with the slaves in Egypt? Very badly indeed. King Rameses, the mighty builder, having made peace with the Hittites, was able to give the more attention to the enormous building works, the store cities of Pithom and Rameses (*ch.* i.) for storing arms and provisions of war, the canals from the Nile to irrigate the land, the great wall of Egypt along the borders of Goshen. He had an enormous command of human labour, all his slaves and prisoners of war. But he needed them all. They were tasked to the utmost, and doubtless the Hebrews, whom he wanted to crush, were tasked most cruelly of all. A Jewish historian, Philo, who afterwards lived in Egypt, and probably knew the Jewish and Egyptian records, tells us that the taskmasters

51

"became daily more and more savage, like wild beasts in human shape, with hearts as adamant, making no allowance for any shortcomings." And the result was, he says, great mortality, the people perished in heaps; the slave settlements were like a city of the plague, where the dead were cast out upon the desert land to be devoured by wolves and jackals. An awful master indeed was Rameses II. A famous French explorer says, "There was not a stone in his monuments that had not cost a human life," and he adds that it gives one a thrill of horror to look at his mighty erections and to think of all the thousands of captives that must have died under the lash to gratify his insatiable vanity. And the worst of it was that he had a long reign of sixty years.

At length he died. Perhaps the slaves hoped for some relief then. Did they get it? (Exodus ii. 23, etc.). "Cried by reason of the bondage." The new Pharaoh Merenptah was no improvement on his father. He too was a builder. Dr. Petrie in exploring Tanis found this king's name, too, cut on the pillars and sphinxes. But his work is very inferior and in execrably bad taste. So the great national works went on, the taskmasters still plied their whips and the cry of the poor children of Abraham "came up unto God." (*ch.* ii. 24). Poor creatures! how hopeless they grew, wondering was there any God or did He care at all. Doubtless some faithful hearts still trusted and hoped and perhaps crept off at night to Joseph's grave to think of his brave prophecy and to pray and cry to God. But most of them lost heart and joined in Egyptian idolatry. (See Joshua xxiv. 14; Ezekiel xx. 5-9.)

Had God forgotten them? How little they thought

that at that very time on a lonely mountain, 500 miles away, the coming Deliverer was bowing down before God and listening to Him telling what? "I have *seen* their affliction, and *heard* their cry, and *know* their sorrows, and am come down to deliver them." How differently they would have felt if they had known that! Anybody like them now? When big sorrow comes or pain or sickness or some dear one dies, is God looking or caring? How much happier for us if we could believe in God behind it all, caring and pitying and wanting to bring blessing out of the sickness and pain—if when the Church is afflicted we should remember her Master is watching, if when one dies we could look into the beautiful Waiting Life where our dear one is nearer to Christ's presence than ever. Don't you think we should gain greatly if we had more faith in God?

§ 2. The Secret Slave-Meeting

Now after all these years comes a vague rumor through the brick-fields and along the great canal about the two old men from far-off Midian with a most startling message. Who? What message? And one, it was said, was that Moses, whose exciting story their aged elders still talked about, the story that had so stirred the slave settlements long ago—when a prince of Egypt, who was one of themselves, had, for their sakes, refused to be called the son of Pharaoh's daughter.

Then came the secret messages from Moses and Aaron to the heads of families. Before going to Pharaoh they must first be sure that their leadership will be accepted by the people. You can imagine the secret gatherings from Zoan and Pithom and Rameses and Memphis, and along the canals—the secret midnight meetings such as slaves must hold away in the desert or in the inaccessible swamps—desperate men assembling at risk of their lives, such as one reads of in *Uncle Tom's Cabin*, or *The Tale of the Dismal Swamp*. Read me the account of one of these meetings (Exodus ix. 29-31). Can't you shut your eyes and imagine the whole scene? the old slaves, the elders of the tribes, with the first dawn of hope in their eyes. Did they believe? Were they glad? How did they show it? Ah! poor wretches, one needs to have suffered like them to understand the goodness of finding out that God cared after all.

§ 3. *The Embassy to Pharaoh*

What is the next step? Embassy to Pharaoh. Pharaoh was dangerous to approach—held power of life and death—was worshipped as a god. Were they not afraid to face him? Why not? Because God had sent them there, and God was responsible. What a power it gives one to have faith, to believe in God, to know that you are on God's path, and that nothing else matters much. That is the lesson taught us of the two old men standing up fearlessly in God's name against the most powerful king in the world. Can people act thus now? Give instances. Schoolboy kneeling down at night among sneering comrades. Business man or politician or clergyman saying or doing things greatly unpopular because he feels it his duty. No cringing, no yielding, where God's will is concerned, "Whether it be right in the sight of God to hearken unto you more than unto God judge ye." (Acts iv. 19).

Do you think Moses knew that he was risking his life? Do you think he was anxious about that? No. But something else he was anxious about? Lest he might injure the cause of the people. He felt he was an awkward speaker; that unless Aaron could say out well what was needed it would not be said at all. So he kept in the background. Aaron took the lead and made the speech for him. Yet which of the two was the greater and nobler man? So you see it is not mere fluent speaking, but faith in God and self-sacrifice that makes men great and noble.

§ 4. God's Gentleness Towards Egypt

Tell me Moses' first demand. Did he at first demand that Pharaoh should set free all this crowd of useful slaves and all their cattle and property? Afterwards he did—but now he only asked what? That was much easier and more reasonable. And if Pharaoh had done that probably the whole course of the story would have been changed.

Remember then that God dealt gently with Pharaoh at first. You see God had to care for Pharaoh's good and Pharaoh's training, as well as for that of Israel. Many people read Old Testament history as if God cared nothing for Egyptians or Canaanites—only for Jews. Is this right? No. Scripture carefully read teaches that it is not. It tells of God speaking in dreams to Laban and Abimelech. It tells of Melchizedek in heathen Canaan, and Jethro in heathen Midian, and Jonah in heathen Nineveh, and Job in heathen Arabia, and Balaam in heathen Mesopotamia—worshippers and priests and prophets of God. So we read of Confucius in China and Buddha in India, teachers of unselfishness surely taught by God, though their teaching is now so corrupted. And in this very Egypt long before Moses we have marvellous records of God's revelation to the conscience of the nation. We have found their ancient *Book of the Dead*, with its wonderful teaching about justice and righteousness and purity—life after death and judgment of men according to their deeds on earth. Do you think that could come except through God helping them? So if people think that God was the God of the Hebrews only and did not care for the Egyptians they cannot understand aright Old Testament history. Most of the Israelites thought thus. Even the inspired writers in these early days did not get free from this national bias.

God began gently. How did Pharaoh respond? Flung back the suggestion angrily. Who is Jehovah that I should obey him? *I,* the Pharaoh, the child of the Gods! Pharaoh was not an ignorant heathen. The religious books of his nation, especially the *Book of the Dead*, taught of a righteous God who insisted on justice and kindness, even to slaves. That was, I think, why God was so stern with him. He was sinning against light. His own will was the only will he would trouble about. And therefore he gradually lost all sense of a righteous will of God over the world.

Well, he learned by-and-by that God had other ways of talking to him if gentleness failed. What? The ten plagues, the death of his son, the drowning of his host. But for the present he could defy God. "What care I for God? These are my slaves—let them to their burdens." I think he even claims Moses and Aaron themselves as his by right—sons of a slave. "Get *you* to your burdens," he says.

§ 5. Moses' Disappointment, The Store Chambers of Pithom

Surely this was a disappointing end to their interview with the king. But worse was to come before evening. For Pharaoh's anger at their audacity grew hotter when they were gone, and he determined to punish them by increasing the sufferings of the slaves. *He* would teach them to take liberties with the Pharaoh!

What terrible order did he give? (*vv.* 6-9). "Supply no more straw for the bricks! Let them gather straw or stubble! But demand the full number as before!" What did they do? How did they plead with him? Was it any use? No. "Ye are idle; ye are idle. I'll soon teach you to come talking about sacrifices to the Lord your God."

A most interesting confirmation of this whole incident seems to have come in modern days. I told you how M. Naville discovered the store city of Pithom, which the Israelites were building for Pharaoh. From the inscriptions amongst the ruins he discovered that the god of the city had been Tum, and that its religious name had been Pi-Tum the abode of Tum, which corresponds with the Hebrew Pithom. The founder of the place appeared to be King Rameses II., the Pharaoh of the Oppression, and it had evidently been built as a fortified military storehouse or granary in which provisions were gathered for the use of armies or caravans bound across the Eastern desert. ("Treasure cities," Exodus i. 11, should be translated "store cities.") The bricks were composed of the common material, Nile mud mixed with chopped straw, but in places the bricks are apparently made with stubble or of mud alone, without straw or stubble.

So this was the sad result of Moses' effort to help them, "The people were scattered abroad throughout all the land of Egypt to gather stubble instead of straw."

Poor slaves, after all their hopes! How natural it was that they should turn on Moses in their bitterness of soul. What did they say? (v. 21). Oh, it was terribly hard on Moses. Did he retort on them? I am sure he saw there was some excuse for their bitterness. And probably, like men of his type, he put the blame on himself; that he had been too hasty or made some mistake; that it was his fault. What did he do in his disappointment? Rushed off to be alone with God. He remembered all his doubts and fears at the Burning Bush about his ability and about his eloquence. And now, in his misery, he struggles with the Lord. "Oh, God, why did You send me? why did You send me? I am an utter failure. Thou hast not delivered Thy people at all."

Moses in his bitter disappointment rushed to pour out his soul before God, like a child hurt, running to his father at once. So the Psalmists, the Prophets, the Apostles, the Lord Jesus Himself in His trouble and care about men, "continued all night in prayer to God." The most helpful habit we can ever form is the habit of Moses when trouble was upon him. He "complained unto the Lord."

NOTES

IV. 19, *In Midian*. It would seem, therefore, that Moses did not set off at once, but waited for this fuller intimation that the time was come.

IV. 21, *I will harden*. See Lesson VII on the hardening of Pharaoh's heart.

IV. 22, *My firstborn*. In numberless inscriptions the Pharaohs are styled "own son" or "beloved son" of the deity, so Pharaoh would easily understand the meaning.—See *Speaker's Commentary*.

In two papyrus documents of about the date of Moses, found in Egyptian tombs, one passage says, "I have no one to help me in making bricks, no straw," etc., and another tells of twelve labourers punished for failing to make up their daily tale of bricks. This shows how thoroughly Egyptian is the story of Pharaoh and his slaves here.

QUESTIONS FOR LESSON V

How were things going on in Egypt during this time?

Tell of the secret slave meeting in the brick-fields.

Who was with Moses in the embassy to King Pharaoh?

They asked only a small request at first. What?

How did Pharaoh receive it?

Tell of Moses' complaint to God. What lesson has this for us?

What do you know of the store cities Pithom and Rameses?

LESSON VI

THE CONTEST WITH PHARAOH

Read Exodus VI. 1-12.

VII. 14-25.

§ 1. How God Encouraged Moses

Recapitulate. Last chapter closed with failure, disappointment, humiliation of Moses. Is that always bad for a man? Had it happened before to Moses? Yes. Flight to Midian. Was that bad for him? So here—more of God's discipline and training. But very hard? He had taught the people to trust him, said he was their deliverer—that Pharaoh would have to submit. And now he stood before them convicted of failure. Pharaoh had conquered him and ordered him to the brick-fields himself, as a man would a dog to his kennel. And he had only made things worse for the poor slaves. Oh, it was a sore disappointment.

And Moses in his agony of soul could not see what we can now see, that it was necessary for his great life-task to trample down self altogether, all self-esteem, all pride in his miracles, all delight in popular enthusiasm for him, everything that a popular leader loves most.

One thing Moses did know, that it was well to rush off to God to tell Him and to plead with Him. Did he get any encouragement? See all that glorious crowding of promises (*vv.* 6, 7, 8), all the *"I wills."* Do you wonder how God appeared to him? Perhaps in a vision, perhaps as in Midian. I wonder if Moses associated the thought of God's presence only with the solitudes of Midian and the silence of the great mountains. If so he soon finds that God is as close to him in the crowded city and among Egyptian temples—that God is close around men always, and any special miraculous manifestations are just the unveiling for a moment of the *Presence which is always there.*

From this forward he rises from faith to faith, growing more convinced that he has at his back the Almighty God who hates oppression and demands justice and mercy and fair play for the poor slaves who have none to help them. So he cares no more about the sneers of Pharaoh. He is ready for the contest with him, though diffident about himself.

§ 2. The Contest Begins

Very soon the contest begins (*ch.* vii. 15-25). Try to make a picture in your minds. Pharaoh with his proud array of guards and priests and courtiers "goes forth unto the water," down through the streets of Tanis and the long avenue of sphinxes to the River Gate, probably to perform the sacred rites to the mysterious Nile which Egypt worshipped as a god. Little wonder. Remember what the Nile was to Egypt. The whole wealth, the very existence of Egypt depended on it. And to the simple people it seemed so mysterious—every winter running low and clear in its channel—every spring at a certain date strangely, mysteriously, like a living thing rising with its wealth of water to enrich the land. Little wonder they loved and delighted in it and paid divine honours to it. Here is the mystic hymn to it from a manuscript of about Moses' time:—

> "Hail to thee, O Nile!
> Coming in peace, giving life to the land.
> Overflowing the gardens created by RA.
> Coming from Heaven, watering the land.
> Giver of corn, lover of good.
> Hail to thee, O Nile!"

Perhaps this was chanted that day in that Nile procession as Pharaoh "went forth to the water." But before any rites of worship could begin there was an unexpected interruption. What? Yes, Moses and Aaron, whom he had ordered out of his presence as dogs to their kennel, are standing before him again. Are they timid or cringing? As a king to a king, Moses addressed him. "The Lord sent me to thee . . . and thou hast not hearkened. Now thus saith the Lord, In this shalt thou know that I am the Lord. Behold, I will smite the waters in the River, and they shall be turned into blood, and the fish shall die, and the River shall stink, and the Egyptians shall loathe to drink," etc.

You may guess what this would mean to Egypt, and you can guess, too, what the contemptuous answer of Pharaoh would be. Then what happens? Yes. The river is struck in the presence of the dumbfounded king and his train of priests and courtiers, and straightway the sacred water, pure and life-giving, became a horrible mass of blood and rottenness, and the fish that were in the river died, and the river stank, and there was blood throughout all the land of Egypt. The horror of it can be but faintly conceived except in a land with a blazing sun overhead, festering and corrupting. But there was a worse horror. What? That it should fall on the Sacred River. The River was no god after all! This Lord who was ordering kindness and fair play to the slaves was actually the Lord and Master of that River on which the very life of Egypt depended. At a word He could turn its waters into blood and slay its fish. That was a tremendous lesson for Egypt and Israel. The God who through Moses spoke to their conscience was the God that ruled over nature. The God of Right was the God of Might.

§ 3. *Judgment on the Gods of Egypt*

Enumerate some of the other plagues. Now turn to the verse, *ch.* xii. 12, "On all the gods of Egypt I will execute judgment." Notice especially the plagues chiefly fell on the sacred divinities. The Nile was a god. The cattle on whom the murrain fell were sacred—the sacred ram, the sacred goat, the black bull of Apis that was worshipped in Pharaoh's great temple in Tanis; the plague of darkness would make them think that RA, the sun-god, was fallen from the sky. The plague of flies is supposed to be of beetles, one of the most sacred symbols of Egypt. The frog was worshipped as the sign of fruitfulness, and now it was turned into a horror, so that people could not walk without trampling it into a loathsome mass.

You have to think of all this to realize the awfulness and the horror of God's judgments on Egypt. "Who is Jehovah that we should obey Him. We have our own gods." And this is Moses' tremendous reply in the plagues. The God of Righteousness—the God of conscience, the God who commands you to be fair and just and kind to these slaves—that is Jehovah, and all these poor gods of yours are but His creatures which He uses to bless the world, and which He can turn into a horror and abomination in a moment.

§ 4. Egypt's Knowledge of Religion

Now I want you to see that God's stern teaching by Moses should have been easily understood by the Egyptians. For God's Holy Spirit had not neglected Egypt. I told you before that their sacred books taught them about one God who was supreme above all—who judged men righteously and weighed their souls in great scales of judgment. And though they worshipped the sun and the Nile and the sacred beasts, yet the wise and good amongst them taught that these were only forms or manifestations of the One Supreme God.

Fifteen hundred years before Moses they had a

knowledge of God of which the monuments and writings that remain to us bear witness. A great German student of the old inscriptions declares that ancient Egypt had a knowledge of a God of Righteousness, little, if anything, inferior to that of the Hebrews of Moses' day. Here is some of their teaching long before Moses:—

> "God is one and alone and none other is with Him.
> God is the One who hath made all things.
> God is eternal, enduring for ever.
> No man is able to seek out His likeness.
> God is truth, and liveth by truth.
> God is love, through Him alone man liveth.
> He breatheth the breath of life into his nostrils."

And again—think of it in Pharaoh's oppression of Israel:—

> "God is merciful to them that fear Him.
> He heareth those that call upon Him.
> He protecteth the weak against the strong.
> He heareth the cry of one bound in fetters.
> He judgeth between the mighty and the weak."

So you see that God had not neglected Egypt and taught only Israel—that Pharaoh and his Egyptians, in spite of all their degrading idolatry, had at least some glimpse of a great, supreme, all-holy God, Master and Chief of all that they worshipped. So when Moses brought a message of Righteousness and Mercy for the slaves— and when he showed that his God who sent him had power over all the idols of Egypt, they might easily have guessed that the supreme God, who speaks in man's conscience, whom their ancient books of religion told of, was dealing with them. You must remember that, if you would understand this history. In next chapter we shall talk more about these plagues and see how God's sternness and God's love are both exhibited.

NOTE

VII. 11, etc., *The magicians.* It is not easy to form an opinion as to whether these acts were clever jugglery. Notice that the magicians were not at any time taken unawares, and therefore could prepare themselves. Interesting treatises have been written on Egyptian magic. The books of magic formulæ belonged to the king, and no one was allowed to consult them but the council of wise men or magicians, who were called on by Egyptian kings on occasions of difficulty.

QUESTIONS FOR LESSON VI

Try to picture in words Pharaoh going to worship the Nile and meeting Moses.

Was Moses as much afraid this time after he had prayed to God?

Tell his brave demand to the king.

What did he do to the river? What made this such an awful shock to Pharaoh?

Had the Egyptians the excuse of knowing nothing about God and duty?

What do you know of their religion?

HOW PHARAOH'S HEART WAS HARDENED

Read Selections from Exodus VIII., IX., X.,

or give brief statement of the plagues.

§ 1. God's Sternness and God's Love

Which of these two does the Gospel teach most to us, God's sternness or His love? Which of these two do the Plagues of Egypt most teach? Is there no love shown in them? What! not even to Israelites? In thinking of sternness to Egyptians, remember it was to deliver the poor Israelites—that their cruel oppressors had to be *forced* to let them go.

Some think God ought to be too loving to hurt Pharaoh. Suppose a shepherd so loving to wolves that he let them eat his sheep, or a judge so loving to thieves that he let them rob the honest. Would that be right? So you see there must be sternness in God's love. You remember our Lord's awful sternness to those who would lead astray His little ones. What does He threaten?

(St. Matthew xviii. 6). So God had to be stern for Israel's sake. Any other reason for sternness? For sake of Egypt and Pharaoh. God had to think of their good, too, and be stern, as a father must with disobedient children.

Should a father be very loving to his children? But if he be a mere weak, good-natured, indulgent father, who never punishes—who would do anything rather than let his children cry—would that be good? Why not? So with God—He cares greatly that His children should be happy. But something else He cares much more for? Yes, that they should be good. He will spare them no pain, if pain be necessary for that—just as He spared Himself no pain for it on the day of Calvary.

How long did God's punishments on obstinate Egypt last? *Only so long as they were obstinate.* Every time Pharaoh repented and promised to obey what happened? (*ch.* viii. 8, 28, 29; ix. 27, etc.). And then when God withdrew punishment, what did Pharaoh do? So more punishment came. If Pharaoh had repented and kept his word, do you think God would have kept on hurting him? He knew in his conscience that what God ordered about the slaves was right—and I think if he had obeyed God and conscience, God would have forgiven him and helped him to be a good, noble king. And so I don't think it at all hard or unfair that the heavy punishments should come.

So I want you to believe greatly in the sternness of God. I trust you will believe in God's love to the very utmost. You can't believe that too much. But you must not believe that He is a mere soft-hearted

69

God, of boundless, easy good-nature, no matter how people behave. People must not take liberties with God or with His everlasting laws of right and wrong. There is boundless love and forgiveness for those who want to repent and be good, but there is boundless punishment for those who do not want to repent and be good. Boundless punishment, i.e. *so long as* they do not want to repent and be good. Do you think that is contradictory to God's love? All obstinately godless people are injuring God's world, their wrong words and deeds are injuring and hurting and leading astray God's poor strugglers, and so in love God must be stern.

§ 2. How God Hardens Hearts

But though we can believe that God must sometimes be stern, there is another thing said that we find very hard to believe. What? (*ch. xi. 10*). Can we believe that God would harden a man's heart to make him sinful, and then punish him for hardness of heart? Why cannot we believe that? Because our conscience, which is given to us by God, shrinks from such a thing. It seems to us unfair, and God in our conscience is always declaring to us that no one must be treated unfairly. Right must be done to every man, to Pharaoh as well as to the Israelites. You are quite right, therefore, in feeling puzzled at the statement that God hardened Pharaoh's heart.

But how can we explain it? It is not easy. We find the hardening mentioned twenty times. Ten times it is said that God did it, and ten times it is said that Pharaoh himself did it. This sets us thinking. What would you gather from it? Surely, that there are two sides to this hardening, and that Pharaoh himself must be at least in some measure responsible for it. Let us try to understand this.

First tell me what Pharaoh had within himself that should help him to obey God in being merciful to the Israelites? His conscience. And you remember I told you of the religious teaching in Egypt that should help his conscience. This teaching told of One Just and Merciful God, supreme over all, and of the duty of men to be righteous and merciful. Here is an old Egyptian prayer that I did not tell you of before:—

> *"O grant that I may come to Thee.*
> *I have not sinned—I have not borne false witness.*
> *I have given bread to the hungry.*
> *I have given water to the thirsty.*
> *I have given apparel to the naked.*
> *I have given a boat to the shipwrecked.*
> *Therefore let it be said to me,*
>
> > *Come in Peace."*

So you see that Pharaoh's conscience and his religious teaching would show him that cruelty was wrong and that he ought to be merciful to the poor slaves. But when the voice of Conscience said, "You ought," what did Pharaoh reply? "I will not." Did that ever happen in your life? Did you ever refuse to do what Conscience told you? Do you know what happens then? The heart each time gets a little bit hardened, and if you go on for a long time it will get very much hardened. This is the law of Conscience which I want you to learn:—

"Every time the voice of Conscience is obeyed it becomes clearer and more distinct next time. Every time it is disobeyed it becomes duller and lower next time and the heart grows harder."

Repeat that again. That is the law of Conscience in all men. Who made that law? Who made Conscience to harden the heart like that after disobedience? God. That is the punishment He has set for disobedience. So you see in one sense it is God who thus punishes us by this hardening. So you might say, "God does it." Yet the man does it himself. Suppose a farmer sows his field with seed of thistles. Thistles come and spoil the field. Who made them grow in that field? God did; for it is He who gave the seed life and power of growth, and gave air and moisture and sunshine to it. But is God to blame for having thistles in the field?[1]

Now try and tell me in your own words how Pharaoh hardened his heart and yet it might be said God did it. Yes. Now, is that true of you and me too? Do you know it frightens one to think of that awful law of Conscience? I want you to remember it always and be frightened at it. It is an awful law of God. Does God, then, say, "There is My law of hardening, and I don't

---

[1] I am quite conscious that a thoughtful reader may retort: "Why, then, did not the writer of Exodus put it thus, and not tell us with brutal frankness that God hardened Pharaoh's heart?" I don't know. I doubt if the writer of Exodus would have felt our difficulty at all. He lived in a much earlier stage of God's education of the race. It is the teaching of Christ that makes it incredible to us that God should treat Pharaoh in a way that seems to us unfair. I doubt if the writer of Exodus would see any difficulty in treating an enemy hardly.

care whether you harden your heart or not"? Oh, no! God is greatly sorrowful if our hearts get hardened. God has done everything He could to make them get soft instead of hard. Remember warning in *Venite*, "To-day if ye will hear His voice, harden not your hearts." God's messages of good are always coming to us, and must be either hardening or softening us.

§ 3. How God Softens Hearts

What do you think God does to soften hearts? Once I read a strange old story of a king in some ancient land whose dominions were greatly disturbed by the committing of a certain crime. At last he made a law that the next man brought before him and found guilty would be punished with the loss of his eyesight. So one day, seated on his judgment seat, he heard the tramp of soldiers, and a disguised prisoner was brought in before him bound. He had committed this crime; there was no doubt about it. Nothing to do but give judgment. But as the old king rose in his place, the prisoner raised his head and the king saw it was his own young son, whom he dearly loved. What was he to do? There came the great temptation to break the law and let his boy free. But he was a good and righteous king, so he could not do that.

There was a long, awful pause, and then quietly and solemnly the old man arose and came down from his place and stretched himself on the iron bed where the criminals were tortured. The executioner stood by with the red-hot iron to deprive the prisoner of his sight. "Put it on my eyes instead!" said the old king. They were all horrified, but they dared not disobey. The red-hot iron passed across his face, and when he rose up stone-blind, the prisoner and the whole court stood silent as death. And then he turned to his son. "My boy, you are free now," he said, "your punishment has been borne. You will be a better man in the future." Don't you think that if anything in the whole world could touch that young man's heart, that would? I do not say that this is exactly what God has done for us, but it is very like it. When and where did He do it? That is God's way of softening our hearts. Now will you try and explain to me again what God does (against His will) to harden men's hearts, and what He does (with His will) to soften them?

So you see you must keep the two sides of God's character together—the sternness and the love—if you would understand Him. He who punished Egypt so terribly is He who came to seek and save that which was lost. He who sent death on the firstborn children of Egypt is He who took the little children in His arms and blessed them. He who overthrew the power of the mighty Pharaoh is He who was "led as a lamb to the slaughter" to save poor sinners from their doom.

QUESTIONS FOR LESSON VII

Name some of the ten plagues.

Was it cruel of God to send them?

Would God have continued them if the Egyptians had repented?

How do you know?

Does God do anything like this now to people? Explain.

We read that God hardened Pharaoh's heart. Would it be fair of God to harden a man's heart and then punish him for that hard heart?

Here is a very difficult question: the Bible says that God hardened Pharaoh's heart and also that Pharaoh hardened his own heart. Could you explain?

LESSON VIII

THE NIGHT OF DELIVERANCE

Read Exodus XII. 1-39.

§ 1. *The Threatened Punishment*

Recapitulate. Give list of plagues? How did Pharaoh behave during plagues? Now keep in mind that Moses began gently, with an easy demand—that the oppressors were warned of the plagues beforehand—that the plagues only gradually increased in severity—that every time they repented the plague was withdrawn, and every time it was withdrawn they withdrew their repentance. So Pharaoh was growing very despicable; a coward when he was in danger, a bully and promise-breaker when danger removed.

At length, as they continued hardening their hearts through more plagues, there came at last the final terrible threat to Egypt. What? Yes. "Every firstborn in Egypt shall die, from the firstborn of Pharaoh," etc., etc. Think of the terror of that threat to the fathers and mothers in Egypt. Don't you think it extraordinary that they should dare to harden their hearts in face of that? Nine times

76

already judgment had been threatened, and nine times the judgment had unfailingly come. Perhaps things did not seem so bad now that they were over and the land was recovering itself; or they thought they could repent again and escape as before. So they hardened their hearts and hoped things somehow would come right. Just what men do to-day when future result of evil-doing is pointed out. That is why the story is so valuable to us. Human nature is the same in days of our own as in the days of King Pharaoh, and God and God's dealings with men are of the same kind. God is behind American and English history, so He was behind Egyptian history, and so from the warnings of that day we must learn lessons for our own day.

§ 2. Waiting for the Blow

How long do you think was occupied by the nine plagues? Perhaps a year or so; at any rate, many months. Probably months elapsed between warning and infliction of the last plague, and no one knew the exact time it would fall. Was Moses to inflict it? No; see *ch.* xi. 4, 5. Picture the interval. Nine plagues come and gone, and the terrible tenth still in the future.

Ever noticed the dread sullen stillness of pause before thundershower? Like that—the two peoples waiting. The Egyptians in doubt and perplexity, not knowing when or whence this dread terror would strike them; the Israelites—how do you think they felt about it? Perhaps a little frightened, but on the whole confident and hopeful, with increasing trust in God, who hates oppression, and in their great leader sent by God. Don't you think they were exciting times in Egypt those weeks of waiting?

Week after week passed in anxious suspense. Then in some way Moses had another Divine revelation. The month Abib, our April, was approaching. This month shall be in future beginning of year. This year the beginning of history for the nation. The day of Freedom is near (*ch. xii.* 1, 2).

Then came the strange awesome directions which Moses repeated briefly to people. (Read *vv.* 21-24.) Choose a lamb on the 10th, kill it on the 14th, sprinkle blood on door-posts; then get in to their huts and shut tight the doors, for the dread pestilence should pass through whole land at midnight of 14th, and all the first-born should die—except? except those guarded by the blood. Pharaoh's own boy should die. In the terror of that night Pharaoh and his people would thrust them out with haste, and that night should be for Israel the birthnight of the nation. Do you think any other nation ever got such an extraordinary message? Describe the extraordinary way in which they were to show their faith in God's promise. Most wonderful exhibition of faith. This horde of poor slaves, whose powerful masters had absolutely determined not to let them go—when they had shut the blood-marked door—were to do what? Dress in travelling order, with loins girded, shoes on feet, staff in hand, ready to go away at the word of command into their unknown future. And thus girded, at midnight, when the awful blow was falling outside, they were to stand round the table eating of the paschal lamb, ready for the start. Were ever such directions given to any nation in the world beside? Is it any wonder that their whole after history is full of the references to it?

§ 3. *The Night of Deliverance*

Now shut your eyes and make this picture in your minds. The night of the 14th. I see the inside of a slave hut. The group round the table, girt for a journey—baggage packed, kneading-troughs on shoulders, staff in hand, eating hastily. I see them trying not to be frightened—trying to force themselves to have faith in God, with the shuddering feeling over them that the Plague Angel was just passing. Then I hear shouts and cries outside, and then a united wild wail of agony ringing out on the midnight through the whole land of Egypt. That startles them. I see the father uneasily watching his firstborn, the mother stooping to listen to the breathing of her baby, the frightened sisters clinging to their brothers, the silent breathless terror as they wait for the dawn. *(Pause.)* And then the great sigh of relief as the midnight passes and the grey dawn appears through the windows, and they timidly venture to open the blood-stained door, and they hear the neighbours whispering that all are safe; and they see then the frightened hope is changed to trusting certainty, and all over the slave quarters of Goshen has been learned the first great lesson of religion—what? "Have faith in God." The most necessary of all lessons for them just then. Could there be a better way of teaching it?

Oh, what a wonderful night it was, that birthnight of the Israelite nation. What does the Bible say of it? (*v.* 42). "A night to be much observed unto the Lord." No wonder the whole history of the Jews is stamped with the memory of it. No wonder that this very year and every year the descendants of the Israelites, wherever they are to-day—in America or England or Germany—have been repeating at Easter-time that old Passover celebration. Something like that scene that you have just been picturing will be enacted next Easter all over the world wherever there are Jews. Things do not thus get stamped into the memory of a people and continue for 3000 years unless they really occurred and made a deep impression long ago. In next lesson we shall see how this story belongs to us all, Christians and Jews. But just now we must go on with the history of that night.

§ 4. *The Gathering of the Tribes*

Think of the excitement all through that night, and from early dawn the sounding of trumpets, the gathering of the tribes from Memphis and Tanis and Tel es Maskouteh and the Wall of Egypt and the Works at the Canal. Six hundred thousand men, besides women and children, moving towards the appointed meeting-place at Succoth. How cleverly Moses must have planned it all beforehand.

In the late war the most difficult thing was the handling of great bodies of men and converging them on a given place at the appointed time. How much harder for Moses. Why? All untrained slaves. How well all his old training in Egypt would come in now, the wisdom and prudence and skill in leading men, which he had learned when he led Pharaoh's armies to victory in Ethiopia. Wonderful how God had been training him, though he did not know it then.

It is the most wonderful march in all history. About 100 years ago it was a somewhat similar event: 400,000 Tartars in a single night starting from the confines of Russia to migrate to the Chinese borders. But this March of the Slaves more wonderful still. Why did not Pharaoh stop them? Ah, yes. Pharaoh had something else to think of, with his dead son lying in the palace, and the whole land filled with mourning and the crowds of Egyptian parents clamouring at his gates. What did they cry out? "Send them out, send them out. We be all dead men." (*v.* 33). The whole night was full of dread and excitement in the royal city. What happened next? A hurried council held; a hurried message to Moses from the king. What message (*vv.* 30-32). Ah! that was the complete surrender of Pharaoh. "Rise up. Get you forth. Take your herds and flocks and be gone; and bless me also!" Not much fear of any hindrance to their departure now!

So from early dawn Moses and his officers were directing the march. One band marched off to the tomb of Joseph. Why? (*ch.* xiii. 19). To carry off the mummy of the old dead chieftain, around which their hopes had been clustering for 400 years. Tell me Joseph's prophecy. "God will surely visit you, and ye shall carry up my bones from hence."

§ 5. *Lessons*

What especially do you think the Israelites learned from all this? To have faith in God. What great purpose had God in view for the Israelites? For this purpose what was most important? Surely faith. All this experience would teach them of a great personal God ruling the world, caring for the oppressed, watching men's conduct, loving righteousness—that this God was very near them. This was the gist of their message to the world. They never could believe it or teach it fully unless their own experience had taught them.

Do you think Pharaoh with his dead son in the palace that night was thinking of God as good, and kind, and righteous? Surely not. It is an awful pain to lose one's firstborn son. But would his hard thoughts be justified? First remember God had warned him, but he would not yield. He forced God to send the punishment. But beside that, if Pharaoh could but know it, that young prince and all these Egyptian children were but removed into the great Waiting Life beyond the grave, with probably far better surroundings and chances of being good. Many a man since Pharaoh has lost his son by sudden stroke like that without thinking hard thoughts of God. For beyond the veil in that Waiting Land the dear ones are alive in God's presence, God's blessed training and discipline are around them. They are not dead—they have lost nothing for which we loved them. We may love them still and look forward to the hope of meeting them. Perhaps Pharaoh did not know it. But God did. And, therefore, we who know it too will understand that things which men think hard and cruel of God are not necessarily so.

QUESTIONS FOR LESSON VIII

What was the last and worst of the plagues?

Would God do that if He could help it?

To show this tell what had happened after each of the plagues.

Try to make a picture in words of that awful night of the Deliverance.

What was the mark that saved the Israelite families?

What does it remind us of in our religion?

Tell of the march of the slaves.

LESSON IX

THE PASSOVER

Read parts of Exodus XII.

§ 1. *The Sprinkled Blood*

Recapitulate the last lesson. We have been thinking of the historical fact of Israel's deliverance. But there is something to ask before we go on. Do you think there was any meaning, any lesson for us in the peculiar ceremonies ordered, the slain lamb, the blood sprinkled to save the people, the memorial established for all generations? Do you think it pointed forward to some other great fact? What did it teach? The Lamb? The Passover Memorial?

I do not mean to say that the Israelites recognized all this meaning. I think that all they learned here was that God chose this curious means, a slain lamb and sprinkled blood, for their deliverance. They did not understand about the Lord Jesus and His atonement that was to be. There was a dim prophecy of it in Eden (Genesis iii. 15). Then this strange order about the lamb and the blood. Then later prophecies (see Isaiah liii. 7).

84

Then all through the New Testament we find our Lord spoken of as the Lamb of God, the Lamb that was slain, etc. *(Get Concordance and work out this more fully.)* So as we think of all this and see how our Lord was slain for the deliverance of the world, we cannot help thinking that God meant here to shadow forth the Atonement on Calvary. You remember our story (Lesson VII) about the old king? That helps us a little towards understanding. Do you think that young man would have been so touched by his father's love if the king had said, "Never mind the law or the punishment appointed, you may go free"? No, that would be a bad lesson for him and for all. They would think they could do wrong more safely again. So it would be bad for us. But God said, My sinful children have brought this sad result on themselves. What can I do with them? I can't bear to let them perish; I must go down and suffer for them that they may be set free, and may be touched in their hearts, and hate sin for ever. We can't here explain all about the Atonement. Only we know that in some way it was necessary that our Lord should die, that His blood should be shed for our salvation. Now tell me how Israelite story was a sort of picture of ours. Point out, (1) The plague was ready to fall on all, both Egyptian and Israelite; (2) God provided a way of escape, and only those who sheltered themselves under the sprinkled blood were safe; (3) Even if Israelite felt frightened behind the blood-stained door, still he would be just as safe. So are we if we come to Christ ever so timidly; (4) They were set free to start on a new life in God's presence, which should end in the Promised

Land. Show how all this is a picture of our condition. So this old story concerns us closely—not merely the Israelites.

§ 2. The Memorial Feast

Now about the remembering of it. Do you think these Israelites who spent that awful night in Egypt would ever forget it? But as years passed by in their new life, and this whole generation of Egyptian slaves had passed away, do you think that their children and grandchildren would remember so well all this that God had done for their fathers? So, to prevent their forgetting, what did God command? Every year, on this same day, a memorial feast, in which they should act over again the fact of their deliverance.

Tell me briefly the directions. How long did they keep it up? Yes, as we saw last day, they keep it up in some measure to our own day. This year and last year the Jews all over the world still kept the Feast of the Passover and Unleavened Bread. (Impress this fact on the class, it will make the story seem less of a vague, hazy, old-world story.) All this was to keep in their memory how God had delivered them by the slain lamb and the blood-shedding. Now I want you to shut your eyes and make three pictures rapidly in your minds.

I

The first Passover in Egypt. Teacher turn back to last lesson. Try to make a vivid word-picture of that scene, the blood-sprinkled door, the frightened group within, the death angel passing, the cry of agony ringing out on the midnight through Egypt, the great sigh of relief as the dawn came and they found all safe, and with deep wondering awe thanked God, and went forth on their new life, resolving that through generations to come they would keep the Passover in memory of their deliverance.

✄ II

We change the scene. Fifteen hundred years later. A Jewish carpenter with his family has come up from the country to keep the Passover in Jerusalem. In the little company round the board is a boy of twelve years old, who has now, for the first time, got a glimpse of the big city and the great outer world that lies beyond his little home at Nazareth.

The feast is begun, far more elaborate than the hurried meal in Egypt. I see the cups of wine pass round the table, and the unleavened bread and bitter herbs, and then the slain lamb is placed before the head of the family—pointing back for those Jews to the slain lamb in Egypt—pointing forward for us Christians to the Lamb of God that taketh away the sin of the world. Now, before the lamb is touched, comes a beautiful part of the Jewish ritual. Amid solemn silence the youngest child rises at the board, and the boyish voice breaks the silence, "What mean ye by this service?" And then the oldest man present rises to reply, "It is the sacrifice of the Lord's Passover, who passed," etc. (Exodus xii. 26, 27).

What curious questions arise as we think of that scene! Who do you think was the youngest boy? (Luke ii. 42). Don't you wonder what were the thoughts in His mind as He watched for the first time that ceremony which for 1500 years had been pointing forward to Himself, and as He asked that question, "What mean ye by this service?" I wonder did the child Christ understand it all and know what was before Him in the future. Who can tell?

✳ III

We change the scene again. Twenty years more have passed. It is evening. The Hebrew boy, now a thoughtful, solemn Man, is again at the feast. Around Him are sad faces of men who for years past had followed Him and loved Him, and who are now wakening up to the meaning of His hints about His departure and His sufferings. Sorrowfully they sit as the first wine-cup passes round, and the bitter herbs are eaten, and the Passover lamb is placed before them on the board. And now great high thoughts press on their Lord's attention. The Jewish Passover is to be done away. He to whom it had pointed for 1500 years, the Lamb of God, is to be offered up to-morrow on Calvary, a sacrifice for the sins of the world. He is to change the Jewish Passover for a new Memorial Feast to keep men in remembrance of His death upon the cross.

So, amid wondering silence, He rises, takes a piece of the unleavened bread, and blesses and breaks it, and gives it to each one, saying, "Take, eat. This is My body which is given for you. Do this in remembrance of Me. After the same manner He takes the cup, saying," etc. (see Luke xxii. 14-20).

§ 3. Holy Communion

So the Jewish Memorial Feast was exchanged for a higher one, and all through the ages since the Church has kept that memorial. Any Sunday in church, as we look at preparation for the Holy Communion, we can go back in imagination, Sunday before Sunday, in one long line of commemoration till we come to that quiet evening in Jerusalem just before His death, and hear our Lord say to His disciples, "Do this in remembrance of Me."

Do you think people ought to do it? If your mother a few hours before she died asked you to come on that day every year and put flowers on her grave in remembrance of her, should you not be ashamed if you neglected it? Even if you could see no use in it but just gratifying her wish? Do you think the same of our Lord's memorial? Even if you could see no use in it, but just because He asked you? But it is of enormous use to us. Not only keeps our hearts touched by the memory of what He has done; but also in a mysterious way that we can never explain communicates to us God's own nature and so tends to make us more like Him.

It is very thoughtless and ungrateful that people should neglect this great memorial of the Lamb of God. And it is very foolish, for they lose such blessing by its neglect. What was done to Jews if they neglected their memorial? (Numbers ix. 13). But now no threat. Only just the Lord's loving words, "Do it in remembrance of Me." When you are older and are admitted to it, don't neglect it or treat your Lord disrespectfully. You will then be taught how to prepare for it. If rightly prepared for and rightly received, it will be the greatest help and blessing of your lives.

QUESTIONS FOR LESSON IX

Do you think those Israelites would ever forget that night of deliverance?

Might not their descendants forget?

What did Moses arrange by God's direction to keep them from forgetting?

Has our Lord done anything like this to keep us remembering His great deliverance?

What do we call His memorial feast?

Can you recall the three Passover pictures in this lesson?

CROSSING THE RED SEA

Read Exodus XIII. 20, etc., and XIV.

§ 1. The Host and Its Leader

Now we resume story from Lesson VIII. Last scene was?—the awful night of Israel's deliverance. The scene opens now on following morning, that famous 15th of Abib, the morning sun shining on the vast hosts gathering in from every direction, from Memphis and Tanis and Tel es Maskouteh to the great "gathering of the Tribes" at—where? Succoth. How many? (xii. 37). What a stirring sight! 600,000 men marching, five in a row (*ch.* xiii. 18). Behind them the wagons of women and children and the vast crush of cattle and baggage and tents choking up all the roads that led towards the desert.

Who was in command and responsible for this crowd? What a burden of anxious responsibility rested on Moses! Show me how his previous life and training had fitted him for it. (1) He had learned calm, strong faith in God. (2) His training in Egypt as a soldier and leader of men. (3) His high character, that made people trust and follow him. It was just forty years since he had made his great life decision for God and Right. Where had he spent those years? And don't you think in all that lonely exile he had been living in close communion with God, growing nobler, truer, more unselfish? I think the reverence for Moses' character made a great part of his power over that unruly host. In his day, as in ours, the man who puts righteousness first and seeks nothing for himself will always be believed in and reverenced.

§ 2. The Pillar of Cloud

All the morning, all the day, the people are pouring out, till the whole converging crowds are assembled as one at—where? (xii. 37). Then on to? (xiii. 20). Etham, on the edge of the wilderness. And as we watch the great march we gradually become conscious of a new mysterious thing in our picture. What? (xiii. 21). Did you ever see dark, strange-shaped clouds forming themselves in sky like castles or pillars or great animals? What was this cloud shaped like? How could they see it at night? Red light of fire shining at the heart of it—sign of God's presence. Where else was God's presence thus shown? (Exodus iii.). So it went on, watching, guiding, protecting.

What was its use? To show them the way to Palestine? I don't think so. Any guide could do that. Joseph's brethren had travelled it easily. Jacob's funeral went along it. No supernatural guidance needed. What then the reason of the pillar? This—God had great designs for the Israelite people. What? To be God's teachers, to keep alive the light of God's truth in the world. And this wretched, degraded slave mob was yet utterly unfit. They needed to be trained and taught and disciplined and shaped into men. They had to be kept in God's presence, in constant dependence on God, till the reality of His presence and His care for men was stamped into their very souls. And so God had to take them aside from the world to prepare them for their mission. As Moses in Midian, as Elijah, as St. Paul, as the blessed Lord Himself, were taken apart for forty days or forty years, or some special period of retirement and preparation—so was Israel. Instead of getting to Canaan in a few weeks, they were to follow the Pillar southward or northward or eastward or westward, in what would otherwise seem the most aimless way— till the whole slave race that came out of Egypt were dead and a new vigorous generation arose, born in the wilderness, trained in the sense of God's presence, trained to be soldiers, some of them to be heroes and saints, in that wondrous, miraculously-guided life that God had planned for them. Don't forget that purpose when you wonder about the Pillar and the forty years' journey.

§ 3. "Between Migdol and the Sea"

On they march, day after day, to Succoth, to Etham, along the edge of the wilderness, following always their miraculous guide, until one night they are surprised to find themselves encamping in a place that even an ignorant man could see was very dangerous. They were marching along the line of cultivated land at the edge of the wilderness until they came facing the great mountain cliffs of Baal Zephon, and heard beside them the murmur of the sea. The sea was at their left hand, the impassable desert sands at their right, and in front of them the mountain cliffs.

If an enemy should follow there was nowhere to escape except into the Red Sea. The people must have been surprised. Perhaps even Moses was. But he was obeying orders—following the guiding Pillar, therefore his mind was calm. It is a great comfort in any danger to feel we are in the path of duty, obeying God's orders. Nothing else gives such calm.

It was all very well at first. No enemy in sight. Pharaoh was busy mourning his dead son. The Egyptians were too frightened after that night of terror. Did this continue? No; as the days passed the terror died away. Then they saw the villages empty, the brick-fields deserted, the great works of Egypt stopped for want of slaves. And the heart of Pharaoh and his servants was turned against the people, and they said, "Why have we done this, to let Israel go from serving us?" And in the midst of the grumbling came the rumours of the Hebrews in their dangerous camp between Migdol and the sea. "They are entangled in the land, the wilderness hath shut them in!" I can imagine the young soldiers of Egypt laughing at the folly of the Israelites, and how the old warriors who had served under Moses long ago would wonder what he meant. At any rate "the Egyptians pursued after them, all the horses and chariots of Pharaoh."

§ 4. Terror in the Camp

You can imagine the rest. One evening, to their horror, the setting sun showed them on the desert hills behind, the horses and terrible chariots of Egypt. How did they behave? Were they brave and trustful? (See xiv. 12.) We can hardly blame them for being greatly frightened. The position seemed most serious, and they had not yet had the wide experience that came later of God's power and watchfulness over them. But still, should not you expect they would trust God and Moses a little now?

Ah! it was a thankless task Moses had. And that was but the beginning of a long series of rebellings and revilings that nearly broke the old leader's heart. Every time anything went wrong, about food, or water, or danger, or discomfort, the wretched creatures were crying and howling, wishing themselves back again in the brick-fields with the "leeks and garlic and onions" of Egypt. Liberty was as nothing compared with gratifying their appetites. God's presence was of less importance than safety for their skins.

How did Moses reply? (v. 13). Was it not fine to see him thus calm and steadfast? Do you think he knew how they were to be delivered? No. He did not know, was in secret crying to God (v. 15). But he knew he was in the path of duty and that when God's leading brings people into danger, God will look after them. A good thing for us all to know that.

95

§ 5. *God's Deliverance*

What was the first startling order? (*v.* 15). What the first miraculous movement towards deliverance? (*vv.* 19, 20). The Israelites were completely in a trap. In front and at the sides the sea, the cliffs, the desert sands, the enemy on the cliffs behind. They could not even move to carry out the plan of crossing the sea if they had known of it, as enemy would swoop down on first sign of such movement. But when the Pillar moved to the rear between the two armies, how did it affect the position? It hid the movements of Israel. In front of Egyptians thick mysterious darkness which they dared not enter. Israelites all night in light, could load their beasts, form in column, get in position on the shore ready for start. But what a solemn awe and dread were on them as they faced the sea!

Now what do you think really happened to enable them to cross? When I was a child I used to picture to myself a great, broad, calm, deep sea with a long, deep, sharp cut made through the middle, so that if you could look over the edge you could see two solid walls of water, and between them, down deep below, the Israelites walking dryshod on the bottom. I saw no reason then, and I see no reason now why God should not perform that miracle if it were necessary. But I don't now think He did. I think what really happened was just as miraculous since it happened by God's will at the critical moment that it was wanted. But I think the miracle that happened was much more natural and probable and in keeping with God's methods than the miracle of my childhood's fancy.

It is generally believed by scholars that the route of the Israelites must have crossed the sea somewhere near the head of the Gulf of Suez, which probably stretched farther inland than now. The probable place, as indicated on the map by the Egypt Exploration Fund, is now dry land, or at least it was until it was cut through by the Suez Canal some years ago. The distance across may not have been more than a mile or two, since the passage of the entire host seems not to have occupied more than a few hours. Now in such cases, unless the water were very deep, a violent landward wind has been known to lay bare the bottom for a considerable distance. For example, history tells us that in 1738 the Turks had the Crimea strongly fortified against the Russians. But in spite of it the Russians got in at the Isthmus of Perekop by a passage made for them by the wind through the shallow waters of the Putrid Sea at the north-west corner of the Sea of Azov. And a still more striking instance is given by a traveller, Major-General Tulloch, who himself saw, *under a strong east wind,* the waters of Lake Menzaleh, in Egypt, recede for a distance of seven miles.[1]

Now it is distinctly stated (xiv. 21) that this miracle was effected by the use of natural means. Perhaps Moses knew that a strong east wind blowing strongly all the night would make the passage quite possible. But of what use would that be unless he could get the strong east wind when he wanted it? This was what constituted the miracle. God sent the strong east wind which opened an escape when all hope seemed lost. Of

[1] See article "Exodus" in Hastings' *Dictionary of the Bible.*

course we cannot be sure, but if that were so, do you think it was one bit less of a miracle than the crossing which I pictured to myself in my childhood?

Now let us look at the account before us and try to imagine the crossing. Was it day or night? How do you know? By the light of fire in the Pillar (xiv. 20, 21). Was it a still, calm night? Read the reference to it in Psalm lxxvii. 15-20, rain, storm, thunder, lightning. Josephus says showers of rain came down from the sky, thunder and lightning and flashes of fire. It must have been an awful night, an awful storm that arose when Moses raised his rod, and the strong east wind, sweeping up like a hurricane, drove the upper waters of the inlet before it landward, while probably the strong ebb tide drew the lower waters seaward so that the bed of the sea lay bare. Still the Egyptians could not see. Their prey seemed safe. At last their watchmen discovered what was happening, and fiercely in the teeth of the storm they swept down on the escaping slaves. (Read xv. 9.) What was the result in the morning watch? (xiv. 24). The wheels sank in the soft sand, the storm kept rising with terrible force. Amid the roar of the hurricane, in the deep black darkness, lit up by the lightning, Moses' rod was raised again and the east wind dropped, and the sea swept back on the ill-fated army of Pharaoh. The Israelites were safe from their foes for ever! The last glimpse we get of them is of a great host of people praising God, singing their joyful *Te Deum* to Him who had delivered them (*ch.* xv.).

§ 6. Lessons

What do you think we learn from this story? There are three lessons:—

(1) The first is taught in the grand *Te Deum* of Moses and the people sung upon the farther shore. Who did they think had won the victory? Yes. Very solemn for them. A well-known historian points out that there are great events in the life of men and of nations brought about by their own exertions, by their own cleverness or holiness. But there are times of higher interest and more solemn feeling when deliverance is brought, not by us, but by causes quite beyond our control; e.g., in English history, the Defeat of Armada—in Jewish history the Crossing of the Red Sea. No Jew could think that anybody but God had accomplished it. How solemn this would make the people!

(2) St. Paul makes this a picture of Holy Baptism. "They were all baptized unto Moses in the cloud and in the sea." (1 Corinthians x. 1, 2). They went down into the water a horde of terrified slaves, they rose up out of it the free, ransomed children of God. Behind them was the land of slavery, in front of them the free and open country, with God's abiding presence to be felt and God's glad, blessed service to be done, and at the end of the road the Land of Promise. It is a picture of the sinner beginning the Christian life. There are many still in slavery to sins and lusts and evil habits. They wish to conquer, but are too lazy to fight, or think it is hopeless. For us, as for Israelites, God provides rescue. "That we

being delivered out of the hands of our enemies might serve Him without fear." (St. Luke i. 74).

(3) Some of us shrink from the drowning of these Egyptians as we did from Death of Firstborn. Why from this more than from other deaths in war or pestilence? Are we afraid that their death must certainly mean eternal damnation too? The Bible says nothing about their future state, only that the firstborn died, that the Egyptians were drowned. We know nothing more except that they did not go out of God's sight when they went out of ours, and that the Judge of all the earth will do what is right and fair and kind to all men. We think, perhaps, many of these soldiers only obeyed orders, and did not deserve eternal ruin. Well, they only passed into the great Waiting Life and God is in that Waiting Life as well as He is here, and God is surely at least as fair and kind and pitiful as we who feel so pitiful about them. Can't we trust them and trust all men with Him?

QUESTIONS FOR LESSON X

Where were those Israelite slaves travelling to?

How long did it take them?

But it could be done in a month. Why did it take forty years?

What guided their journey by day and night all these years?

Now in their journey they got into a very dangerous position. Explain.

Had the Egyptians heard of it? What did they do?

How were the Israelites delivered?

LESSON XI

MANNA

Read Exodus XVI.

Numbers XI. 7-9.

Psalms LXXVIII. 24, 25.

See R.V.

§ 1. The Fright of the Israelites

Remember last scene? The vast host of Israel singing their glad *Te Deum* on the farther shore of the Red Sea, Moses and his warriors chanting the psalm, Miriam and her maidens breaking in with the refrain, "Sing ye to the Lord, for He hath triumphed gloriously; the horse and his rider He hath cast into the sea."

Should not you think they would never cease to remember and thank and trust God after that? What time elapsed before today's story? (*v.* 1). Yet it seems sufficient to make them forget and doubt and rebel just as before the crossing of the sea. What did they murmur for now? Had they begun murmuring before this since the crossing of the sea? (xv. 23). Do you think Moses had a pleasant time as leader? Do you think there was any excuse for the people's fright about food? Of course they ought to have trusted God, but I am afraid we should have been very much frightened ourselves. Why do you think God let them get so frightened? Any purpose in it? Surely it was part of the purpose of that whole forty years' training. By means of this He would teach them—

(1) That they were utterly helpless without God;

(2) That they might trust God for everything.

I think it was because of this discipline that we find so much afterwards in the Psalms and Prophets of the trusting and thanking God. God taught the Israelite people their lessons in a most marvellous way, not by books or classes, but by the wonderful "object-lessons" of experience. Just watch one of these object-lessons to-day.

§ 2. Their First Object-Lesson

Shut your eyes and make a picture. A great, hot dreary desert by the sea—the sun beating down on the hot wastes of sand. A great crowd of men and women and boys and girls—more than in all ____ (mention some large town near you), the children crying for something to eat, the pale, weak women fainting on the ground, the strong, gaunt-faced men looking in each other's faces with a terrible fear creeping over them.

No wonder they were afraid. There were hundreds

of thousands—provisions almost finished, nothing but rocks and stones and barren fields around. What should they do for their wives and little children? What an awful day it was in that camp in the wilderness! So the day went on, and things grew worse and worse, till at length a fierce "bread riot" rose round the tent of the leader. "Bread! Bread! give us bread! Oh, would to God we had died in the plagues! Ye have brought us out of Egypt to kill this whole assembly with hunger!"

Surely an awful picture, an awful responsibility for Moses. What lesson first did I say God wanted to teach?—*That they were utterly helpless without God.* Do you think this would teach it? Can you see any human hope for them, anything they could do to escape? Repeat again before we go on, and keep clearly in mind this first lesson they were learning.

§ 3. *Their Second Object-Lesson*

Now shut your eyes again, continue the picture and find out their second lesson. The same plan, the same murmuring, angry crowd, but a quick change in the scene. Moses, who has been praying to God in his tent, comes out with God's message—and as he comes, the people look to the great Pillar of Cloud on the edge of the wilderness, and behold the glory of a beautiful light is shining on it to comfort them. And Moses speaks to them the message of God. What? "At even ye shall eat flesh, and in the morning ye shall be filled with bread; and ye shall know that I am the Lord."

There is a deep hush, the people listen breathless!

They cease the crying and complaining and begin to hope. They are waiting eagerly, anxiously all the afternoon—four o'clock —five o'clock—six o'clock—no food. The suspense is growing terrible. Then suddenly in the late evening, like a distant cloud approaching, they see a great flight of birds darkening the air and flying low, a great migration of quails, which they can strike down and eat. What a delightful relief! for the present. That is sufficient for the moment. But what of to-morrow and all the morrows? So they go to bed that night not knowing where they shall get their breakfast in the morning, and in the morning they awake, and draw aside the curtains of the tents, and gaze eagerly out, and behold—what? Colour? Taste? Called in Psalms (Psalms lxxviii. 24, 25), "corn of heaven . . . angels' food."

And then they knew God had not forgotten, and they got up wondering and gathered the strange sweet food, just enough for one day. Then they wondered what would happen next day, for that night there was not a particle of food left for that vast crowd. But next morning there was the white bread from heaven again. And so night after night, over and over again for forty years, they had to go to bed without knowing where to get their breakfast in the morning, and morning after morning for forty years—perhaps not always, but as often as it was needed—the white food lay shining on the ground. Now what lesson should that teach them?— *That they might trust God for everything.* Were not these valuable lessons? Was it not a wonderful way to teach them? Repeat together now the two lessons taught them. *(Now get the chapter read, Exodus xvi.— it should not be read before the two picturings—and question the children on the facts of it carefully. Then go on to point out how soon Israel forgot, and how ungrateful they were. Ask—)* "Do you think we should be so ungrateful—so forgetful?" "Oh, no." "Well, I am not so sure. But I shall repeat my question again in a few minutes, and see if you are all of the same opinion. Meantime I want to tell you something like it that happened only last year."

§ 4. *Our Object-Lesson*

I want to tell you not of the Wilderness or the Israelites, but of quite a different place and people that I have been hearing a good deal about of late. It is a large country, not in the East but in the West, of which we have heard a good deal in the newspapers this year, and there are great crowds of people—far more even than in the Wilderness of Sinai. Last year came on them a terrible danger, which reminded me very much of our story to-day. That great crowd were within a few months of being all starved to death. All the food they had was stored up in some shops and barns and storehouses, and would only last till about Christmas. And if something did not happen before that food ran short, this vast crowd of people, like the Israelites in the wilderness, must just wait for a few months and then all die of starvation. Was not that an awful position? And this only last year! Did you not hear of it before? Did you never hear of that country? It has a big town called New York and some mountains called ——— and a river

106

called —— and another town called —— (Here name mountains and rivers and your own town.)

Are you surprised? Most of us thought little about it—but it was true all the same. If God had not done something for us the people all over America would have been dead of hunger, and we should all be lying quiet in the graveyard to-day. You ought to remember that. Every summer the world is within a few months of starvation. It is like as in the giving of the manna. Every day how much could they store up? (Exodus xvi. 19, 20). Only enough for a day. So with us. Every year God, as it were, says to us, "Store up just enough for the year—no more. You will get more next year—you must trust Me for that."

The world has had some sharp lessons to teach this lesson of its helplessness and dependence. You saw the horrible pictures in the illustrated papers of the dreadful Indian famine lately. The writer has heard his father tell of the Irish famine of sixty years ago, of the women dying by the roadside with their babies in their arms, and the fierce starved men wandering through the country seeking for food for their wives and their children. And there it was only one little part of the harvest that failed—the potato crop—and only in Ireland. Think what it would have been if the whole harvest everywhere had failed, and that people in England and all over Europe were unable to send help to any one. So don't you think we should easily learn the first lesson of the Israelites—that we are utterly helpless without God? We are as helpless, waiting on God's bounty, as were the Israelites in the wilderness.

Now what was the Israelites' second lesson? *That they might trust God for everything.* Should we learn that? He saved us last year just as He saved the Israelites that awful day in the desert. What did He do for us? Send us manna? No; but just as great a miracle—sent harvest. Were the people very frightened? What promise had we? (Genesis viii. 22). For countless generations He has fulfilled that. It seems like saying to us every year, "Don't be frightened, my children, I will send you food; My rain and sun and dew will make it grow for you. In July go to your gardens and look under the ground for the potatoes and other crops which I have put there for you, and then go and gather up what I have hung on the fruit-trees for you, and while you gather that I shall be filling your corn-fields for you with the yellow waving corn. Gather it up and eat it up each year. I will send more next year, and next, and next, and every year, because I care for you." Is it not all very like the position of the Israelites? We are just as helpless and dependent on God.

Now I repeat the question that I asked you before— Are we ever forgetful or ungrateful as they were? Therefore we ought to remember at grace before meat and at harvest festival times how much we owe to God and how helplessly dependent on Him we are, and so learn to be very thankful and loving to Him.

That is for our bodies' food. Then for our souls, how does He feed them to make them strong and holy? The Bible is a great nourishment, strengthening us to be good (every child should join one of the children's Bible-reading Unions). Our Lord says (John vi.) that He is the Bread of Life, giving life and strength to all who come to Him for it. This He will do for you if you ask Him. Pray and He will do it for you. And especially in the Holy Sacrament of His Body and Blood when you are older. By this Sacrament, in a marvellous, mysterious way that we cannot understand, He feeds His children and communicates to them of the divine nature that they may grow like God. So for our bodies and souls we may learn the two Israelite lessons—(1) *that we are helplessly dependent on God, and* (2) *that we may trust God for everything.*

QUESTIONS FOR LESSON XI

Recall some of the deliverances of Israel by God.

What should it have taught them? Did it? How do you know?

Try to picture in words the week of their danger of starvation.

How did they behave?

How did God deliver them?

Does anything like this happen to us every year?

How does God deliver us?

LESSON XII

AT MOUNT SINAI

Read Exodus XIX. and XX. 1-17.

Deuteronomy V. 6-21.

§ 1. Scenes in the Desert Life

A new scene again, entirely different from the last. Is it not like magic-lantern changes, the continual rapid altering of the scenes in Moses' life—the palace, the slave huts, the lonely Midian, the night of the dead firstborn, the hurricane on the Red Sea, the joyful *Te Deum*, the starving crowds receiving the manna, etc., etc.

Now a complete change again. We pass to the sixth chapter of Exodus. But in so doing, we have had to pass over a number of other most interesting scenes in chapters xvii. and xviii. After the famine fright and the giving of the manna they came to Rephidim, where there was another fright and murmuring for want of water, and God miraculously supplied their need. Then the famous battle scene, where the tribes of Amalek attacked Israel, and Moses being too old, perhaps, for active fighting, sent Joshua to lead the army, and went up into the hill overlooking the battle-field to pray to God and to hold up his rod. And when he held up his hands Israel prevailed, and when his tired hands dropped Amalek prevailed. So Aaron and Hur stayed up his hands till evening, till Israel had driven off the attacking hosts.

And then we have another most interesting scene (*ch.* xviii.), a picture of Moses' ordinary everyday life when the camp was at rest and there were no battles or expeditions. Such a hard, tiring life. From early morning until late at night he sat to judge and decide and arbitrate and heal disputes and bring the troubles of the people before God, till old Jethro, his father-in-law, coming to visit him and bring back Zipporah, saw that he was likely to break down under the severe nerve-strain. Don't you think that Jethro was right? All the anxiety and responsibility, all the hard work and nervous strain, all the fret and trouble that would come from the continual grumbling and almost rebelling of that ungrateful crowd whenever anything went wrong. "Why did not you leave us alone in Egypt, where we had food enough and water enough and no battles to fight?" "O Lord God," cries the poor tormented leader, "wherefore hast Thou afflicted Thy servant, that Thou layest all the burden of this people upon me?" (Numbers xi. 11). How one's sympathy goes forth to that brave, true heart, bearing all so bravely, sacrificing himself utterly for God and his people!

§ 2. Waiting at Sinai

But to Moses, just now, all these troubles are but minor matters, swallowed up in the far greater things to which he was looking forward, the greatest event in the whole history of the Jews, one of the great events in the whole history of the world. What? Yes; he is leading them to Mount Sinai through the vast mountain ranges that he knew so well in his lonely Midian days. How long now out of Egypt? (xix. 1). All these three months of their training they have been learning God's CARE, God's LOVE, God's POWER. Is that all that is needed to learn about God? What is the supreme lesson? God's HOLINESS AND SIN'S SINFULNESS. That is the lesson now before them.

And all the surroundings seem chosen to impress them with their solemnity. The most impressive, solemnizing scenes on earth are great towering mountain ranges and vast lonely valleys. One cannot help feeling solemn there. The writer vividly recalls one special night in his life, a night in the mountains, in the vast solitudes of the grandest of the Alps. The moon was lighting up the black crags and the great snow-peaks that rose into the sky and the mysterious valleys that stretched away dim and vast at his feet. The solemn impressiveness he can never forget. It was impossible to be thoughtless or trivial there. It seemed just the place where one might expect at any moment to hear God's voice or to see God's glory manifested. It seemed so exactly the fitting place for it. Such was the ground where the Israelites were led. Day after day they penetrated deeper and deeper into those strange, lonely passes. They knew that they were being led there for some solemn purpose, for some great sacrifice or solemn revelation of God. Daily they struggled on under the huge cliffs, over the rugged passes, some by one path, some by another, until at last one day, three months after leaving Egypt, they found themselves all assembled in a sort of great natural temple of the mountains. The huge cliffs of Sinai like an altar in front, the great mountain-peaks everywhere around so solemn and still. God had taken them "aside from the multitude," away from the noise and hurry of life, to be alone with Him for a while in His great temple.

Do you think the people knew exactly what they had come for as they encamped that night? I daresay they had some notion of it. But as they lay there at the foot of the mountain Moses came forth to them from the presence of God with a grand, wonderful message. What message? (xix. 4-7). "If ye will obey My voice, ye shall be a peculiar treasure unto Me above all people; ye shall be a kingdom of priests, a holy nation," etc. What a glorious message for that poor slave race! Don't you think it should touch their hearts in those vast, lonely mountains? Don't you think it touched and lifted up Moses' heart as he received it? What a strange, wonderful life Moses must have been living all this time, with the sense of God's presence and God's purpose so borne in upon him that he must have felt almost like a man in another world!

He told them what they were to do. How long to wait? What directions given as to their preparation? Why the bounds set round the mountain? Why must

113

they stand so far off? Why all this washing and cleansing of themselves? What was the lesson to be taught by all this? GOD'S UNUTTERABLE HOLINESS. Sinful men must not make too free with God. Nothing impure or unholy must come into His presence. You see they might know all about God's power and love and yet think He was but like the gods whom the heathen told of, who did not much care about the purity of men's lives. They must learn that God was of awful holiness. They knew how far from being holy they themselves were, and so this strange teaching seemed to be making them shrink back farther and farther from Him with a new fear, a new shrinking. Was it good thus to shrink back from God? Yes, a very good thing for any man to feel a deep shrinking as he thinks of God's pure holiness and his own deep sinfulness. Some people in our day, who talk rather freely and familiarly about God, and write rather free and familiar hymns, would be the better of feeling more awe and reverence. Some boys and girls would be the better of feeling it when ill-tempered, or greedy, or deceitful, or selfish. Best that they should not feel quite so free and careless as they sometimes do when the evening comes and they kneel down to say their prayers after times of this kind. They should first of all come to Him shrinkingly and sorrowfully, and tell Him sadly about that sin and beseech His forgiveness and His help to keep from such again. Only then can they speak happily and confidently to God in prayer. If people can kneel down lightly or say prayers glibly to God after such days, it shows something very wrong in their ideas of God. We ought to love and trust God—but we should be deeply reverent.

§ 3. How God Came

Three days they waited. What solemn days, washing their clothes clean, trying to keep their souls clean in preparation for God's appearance. Ah! I think it must have done them much good. And all the time their eyes would be on the great cliffs in front, covered with thick clouds, and I suppose they would be wondering in their hearts about—what do you think? What would you be wondering at in such a case? Wondering how God would appear. Would it be as the Hawk or Black Bull in the temples of Egypt? Would it be in the similitude of any figure, the likeness of male or female? What would this All-powerful, All-holy God be like? Thus passed the first night, the second night. Thus the darkness of the third night fell upon the camp, with their expectation wound up to the highest pitch. What a solemn, exciting night! as much so, surely, as that when the firstborn died in Egypt. Do you think they slept much that night?

At last the morning broke in intense excitement, and I can imagine how, in the dim dawn, every eye was strained to see the summit. What is that in the grey twilight dimness? Is it any earthly form, any distinct shape that is unveiling itself? If it were, their passion for idolatry would soon have laid hold of it. Was it? No. There was no form. There were thunders and lightnings and voices, so that all the people in the camp trembled (xix. 16). Long years afterward Moses described the whole scene to the assembled camp. (Read Deuteronomy iv. 11, 12.) "The mountain burned with fire into the midst of heaven, with darkness, clouds, and thick darkness; ye heard the voice of the words, but saw no similitude, only ye heard a voice." That was all they knew, all the impression they were intended to receive. They could not see God; yet they could not help believing that He was there. They were to make no image of the Almighty; yet they were to believe that He was close to them, their Lord and their God.

§ 4. *The Ten Commandments*

And then a very wonderful thing happened. It would seem from the narrative that a clear voice, as of a trumpet ringing through the mountains, pronounced the "Ten Words," or Ten Commandments. We don't quite understand it. It is said (xx. 1) that God spake them. Yet it is said also that through angels it was given (Acts vii. 53; Galatians iii. 19; Hebrews ii. 2).

Of course it would mean much the same if God sent a great angel to utter His commands. At any rate, we cannot speak more positively on the matter. In either case, we may think of the angels as present. What an interest they must take in us! Do you remember at what great times in our history they were present? At the Creation, at the Fall, at the Law-giving, at the chief events of the Old Testament, at the Birth of Christ, the Temptation, the Agony, the Resurrection, the Ascension—all that God was doing for man. And our

Lord says they are so intensely interested in us that "there is joy in the presence of the angels of God over one sinner that repenteth."

Tell me again what God wanted His people to be? (xix. 5, 6). Therefore He began to make them so by giving these laws of right. Why were they to obey them? Was it in order that they should be delivered? No. It was *after their deliverance*. God made no bargain with the poor wretches in their misery. He delivered them freely and lovingly. And then *in gratitude to Him for what He had done* (xx. 2), He asked them to try to be good, to try to do His holy will. Did God greatly care that they should do so? Long years afterwards Moses is telling the people the whole story of the law-giving, and he tells a most touching word of God which is not mentioned here. (See Deuteronomy v. 28, 29.) "Oh, that there were such a heart in them," said God, "that they would fear Me and keep My commandments always, *that it might be well with them* and with their children for ever." Don't you think God cared greatly that they should be good? Was it for His gain or for theirs, "that it might be well with them"? Point out that all this is true for us, too. It "is for our good always" that God wants us to obey Him, and He did not wait until we had obeyed before He laid down His life for us, and received us in infancy into His holy Church. Point out also that these Ten Commandments were very simple, but very deep and full of meaning. Just in their bare literal meaning, they were all that the poor Israelites in their degradation could aim at. But long centuries afterwards, that God who gave them showed His Church how their meaning

117

must be explained and expanded so as to go down into the very thoughts and intents of the heart (Matthew v. 21, 27, 33). In this deeper sense we must understand them.

NOTES

(1) It should be noticed that this Decalogue has in it nothing local, or temporary, or peculiar to one nation. It is a universal law for all mankind. And it is not enforced like other laws, by rewards and punishments. No. It simply makes its appeal to the universal human Conscience. God has made man with a Conscience within him. The great authority of the Decalogue lay in its appeal to this Conscience. People felt bound to obey who did not know or believe anything about the story of Sinai.

(2) With regard to the slight variation in substance of the Commandments as given in Exodus and Deuteronomy, it has been suggested that perhaps all the ten were given originally in the brief form of the 1st, 6th, 7th, and 8th, e.g.—

> "Thou shalt honour thy father and mother";
> "Thou shalt not covet";

and the passages in the longer Commandments in which the variations occur were comments added when the Books were written.—See *Speaker's Commentary.*

QUESTIONS FOR LESSON XII

Do you remember Jethro at Midian? Did he ever meet Moses again?

Where had the Israelites come to when the Ten Commandments were given? Show on map.

What lessons had God been teaching them up to this time? *Answer:* His care, His love, His power. Explain.

Now what great lesson was to be taught? *Answer:* Man's sinfulness and God's holiness.

Try to picture in words the days of waiting at Sinai.

Why does God give these commandments? For His own good or for ours? Explain.

LESSON XIII

HOW MOSES BROKE THE TABLES OF STONE

Read Exodus XXXII. 1-30.

Deuteronomy IX. 9-19.

§ 1. The People's Demand

Show the four sections in the chapter, verses 1-7, 7-15, 15-25, 25-35.

Recapitulate.—Awesome scene in last lesson. The vast crowd on the plain all white and trembling with dread. Above them on the great altar mountain the black cloud, the thunder and lightnings and voice of a trumpet, and the awful miraculous utterance of the "Ten Words" from Sinai. Now read Exodus xx. 18-21; xxiv. 15-18, and think of the old leader going up slope after slope, peak after peak, till at last he reaches the cloud, the pavilion of God. There he unhesitatingly passes within out of sight for forty days and forty nights.

We are only told some of the details of the sad after

120

story. But as we read between the lines we can picture the rest. The tense excitement waiting for him to return. Then the awe and wonder as the days went by and he gave no sign. Then they became uneasy and restless, like children in the dark, with their leader gone and the guiding Pillar absorbed in the dark clouds on the mountain top. "What has happened? Has he lost his way, or died of starvation, or been consumed by the awful presence of God on Mount Sinai?"

And then—what? Yes. Does it not seem almost incredible? That crowd who a few weeks since had heard the miraculous words, "Thou shalt not make a graven image," and had promised, "All that the Lord hath spoken we will do,"—that they should go to make an image of the idol calf of Egypt to worship. How could they do such a thing! The moment Moses' eye was off them they fell. I dare say they would have committed idolatry and worse things fifty times over before this but for his strong hand over them. Now see how they talk of him to Aaron. Repeat their words for me. "As for this Moses," etc. What a wretched, hopeless, ungrateful lot to have to do with! No feeling of what they owed to Moses. No sorrow for the sad fate of their brave old leader. "There is no more to be gained from him, therefore let us forget him!" Does not it give you some idea of what he had to put up with all those forty years? and of what God had to put up with? How solemnly God had taught them of His purity and holiness. And now they are going on to indulge in the filthy orgies of heathen idol-worship. One sometimes hears from missionaries on the African coast of the long years before they can trust their converts, and of the shame and disgrace to the Mission when the passions of the wretched creatures break out. It helps one to understand the sorrow and anxiety of the leader of this Israelitish horde. And this Israelite story, on the other hand, may help us to understand the discouragements of missionary work and the unfairness of the sneers at missionary failures from idle critics sitting comfortably at home.

§ 2. The People's Sin

Which commandment were the Israelites breaking? No. Not the first. Not having other gods. What does second forbid? Making idols, images of God, and so degrading God as if He were like a dead, helpless calf of gold. How do you know it was not some other god they would worship? Verses 4, 5, "which brought thee out of the land of Egypt. . . . To-morrow is a feast to the LORD. They wanted an image like the Black Bull of Egypt. They could not believe in God's presence unless they had something to look at. And I fear also they wanted to indulge in the filthy sinful excesses that accompanied idol feast, where the people used to behave like brute beasts and degrade themselves in the most shameless way.

What do you think of Aaron? Did he sympathize with them, or was he too great a coward to resist them? I think he dared not refuse. He thought of a clever way of getting out of it. What? He said he could not make it without the women's gold ornaments—he thought he knew enough of women's nature to feel sure that they would refuse them. Did they? Then it was too late to take a higher stand. He should have done that at first. What answer do you think Moses would have given? Aye. They might be angry, they might stone him. What would it matter compared with the horror of disobeying God. Look at the shuffling excuse when Moses rebuked him (*vv.* 22, 24). You know the people are set on mischief. They brought me gold, and I only threw it into the fire and there came out this calf! As if the calf had walked out itself. As if he was hardly to blame at all! Even a good man may sometimes be a shuffling coward. A brave servant of God is only afraid of one thing. What? Grieving and disappointing God. Pray God you may be such.

Aaron made the calf, and the people made themselves as beasts in the wild intoxication of their idol feast. When people think their God can be represented by a calf, no wonder they make beasts of themselves in their worship! It happens the same way in Indian idol temples to-day. Men who know Indian idol worship well assure us that its vileness is too horrible to speak of.

§ 3. *The Contrast*

Now turn quickly from this horde of half-naked, brutalized, degraded creatures, yelling and leaping about their idol. Turn quickly to the sharp contrast. Where was Moses all this time? In the pure, holy, calm presence of God. What a wonderful experience! He must have felt like a being of another world.

Of course we cannot conceive what it was—all the unutterable wonder and glory and awe of that forty days. But we can make a faint guess. Did you ever wish to have stood by Christ in Palestine when he was doing and saying such beautiful things to people? Or to get a glimpse into the Unseen Life where some dear one has gone? Or to feel absolutely certain of God's near presence and approval when you were at your prayers or longing to be good—to feel as if He were touching you and saying, "My child, I am helping you"? You can imagine a little of what it meant to Moses, that he should in some measure have got what you often long for, that in some way he should feel the presence of the Holy Loving God as close to him as a man's presence to his friend. Another man once had an experience like Moses'. Who? (2 Corinthians xii. 2, St. Paul is speaking of himself). No wonder the sense of God's presence filled Moses' whole being, and that his face should shine with the reflected glory of it (Exodus xxxiv. 29-35).

Now think of the horrible contrast between that purity and holiness and love—and the filthy, brutal scene going on in the plain. Think of the awful shock when the intimation came to him (read it, *v.* 7). Then at once the chance of a great personal gain came to him—what? (*v.* 10). I do not quite understand this. A strong impression, perhaps, entering his mind that these Israelites were not worth struggling for any longer, and that he might pick out a set of faithful followers himself. I think it must only have been a testing of him, as when Abraham was tempted to offer Isaac. How did he bear the testing? Grandly as Abraham. Selfishness and self-seeking had no part in him now. He had grown too close to the likeness of God.

§ 4. The Anger of Moses

Now I can picture him rushing down, his heart bursting with holy grief and indignation, his hands holding—what? (*v.* 15). Who was waiting for him high up the mountain? Did Joshua know of the evil thing? (*v.* 17).

I can picture the two silently hurrying, Moses too full of his own sorrowful thoughts to speak, when suddenly, as they turn the shoulder of the mountain they are startled by the wild shouting from below. What does Joshua think? Just like a soldier to think that. What did his leader reply? The next turn brings the whole camp full in sight, and a horrible sight it was—the graven image on high with an altar before it, and the brutal half-maddened crowd dancing and yelling, and Aaron his brother in the midst of it all! Oh, it was horrible—and coming from the presence of the pure, holy God it seemed more horrible still. What did he do? Make the picture of it in your mind. The old fierce anger that made him long ago kill the Egyptian slave-driver, burst forth again. Can't you picture the tablets flung down from the cliff. And then—don't you see him starting straight for the camp, his eyes blazing with indignation, and the crowd standing spell-bound, watching him as he comes. Terrified, paralyzed, they stand where he has discovered them. And then can't you see him striding fiercely through the midst, till, all flushed and angry, he reaches the altar, and hurls that wretched image down crashing from its place!

What next? He turns fiercely on Aaron. Did Aaron deserve it? And then? (*vv.* 26, 27). Perhaps he saw signs of resistance or refusal of dancers to cease their debauch. Ah! they had not Aaron to deal with now. "Who is on the Lord's side?" Who came to him? What was his terrible order? Do you think he was right? I do. Remember it was probably only those who resisted and persisted in their sin. Remember our lesson about God's sternness and God's love. There are times when a surgeon must cut into a man with his knife to remove a foul ulcer, and there are times when surgery like that is needed with nations too. Sometimes by one terrible judgment like that a whole nation may be saved from corruption.

But was it great pain to God? Was it great pain to Moses? I am sure it was. I have heard cruel, wicked things said about such deeds as this—that it shows the true attitude of every righteous man zealous for God's honour—that it shows that in the hereafter the saved will be so full of zeal for God that they can think without sorrow of the sufferings of the lost! I think that is a cruel slander on them and on God. Next day we shall see Moses' real feelings as he watched the camp mourning over these new-made graves—we shall see him, with all his holy sternness, full of sorrow and forgiveness, wanting to give up his own life to save those wretched sinners who deserved of him so little. Ah, that is more like the heart of Moses, more like the heart of God as revealed in Jesus Christ.

NOTES

V. 1. Make us gods? should be "Make us a god." The Hebrew word Elohim, though plural in form, is the word commonly used in the Pentateuch to denote the one true God.

Aaron and Hur were left in charge (*ch.* xxiv. 14). The Jews have a tradition that the people first came to Hur, and on his refusal murdered him for his opposition to them, and that Aaron was therefore frightened and yielded.

V. 4. The Israelites were accustomed to the ox-worship of Egypt, and even shared in it while in Egypt (see Joshua xxiv. 14; Ezekiel xx. 8), and therefore it would be easy to fall back into it. Notice when Jeroboam made the calves he used the same cry. These be thy gods, or this is thy god, which brought thee up out of the land of Egypt (1 Kings xii. 28). In both cases the breach was not of the first Commandment but the second.

V. 28. The slain were doubtless those who resisted and persisted in their sin. It was not a general massacre of all who had sinned. Moses gave them all a chance of drawing back when he cried, "Who is on the Lord's side?"

QUESTIONS FOR LESSON XIII

Try to describe this awful breaking of the Commandments. Which of them especially?

What part had Aaron in this?

Where was Moses when it happened?

Tell of his terrible anger and what he did.

Was he right to be angry? Is it ever right to be angry? When? Give instances in our own life.

Could God be pained and angry? How does His anger differ from ours? *Answer:* Pain, stern love, forgiveness if we are sorry.

LESSON XIV

THE GLORY OF MOSES
AND THE GLORY OF GOD

Read Exodus XXXII. 30 etc.,

and XXXIII. and XXXIV. 4-8.

§ 1. Moses' Glory

Read

Last scene ended with the stern judgment on the sin of the people. On whom was it executed? Evidently on those who persisted in their sin. It had to be done, else worse would follow. But did it pain God? Did it pain Moses? We see that by what happened "on the morrow." What? (*v.* 30). The camp was mourning over the new-made graves. The people were miserable in the depression and reaction after their yesterday's sin. Don't you think Moses was very sorrowful for them and longing to have them forgiven and happy? Tell me exactly what he promised? (*v.* 30). "I will go up, peradventure—I know not if I can, but peradventure I shall *make an atonement* for your sin." What is atonement? What do we mean by Christ's atonement?

129

How must atonement be made? *By sacrificing oneself.* What do you think Moses had in his mind when he spoke of making atonement?

The poor, dazed, dejected people listened, but how little they understood the deep purpose in his heart, the price that he purposed to pay! If I understand his purpose aright, I think it is one of the grandest things in the whole Bible story, and, in my mind, lifts up Moses to the highest place among men. Don't you think he had some guess as to the idea of atonement, the innocent suffering for the guilty? The ordinance of the Day of Atonement afterwards (Leviticus xvi.) would indicate that. At any rate I think I know the purpose in his heart as he silently climbed that dread mount in the sight of the people? What purpose? That he would offer himself as a sin offering if God would accept—that he, the prince and leader, would die for the people if God would take his life as a ransom for theirs. Oh, how grandly close to God his life was growing. Only yesterday God had tested him on the top of the mountain. How? (xxxii. 10). By in some way letting the suggestion come to him that he should let Israel be destroyed for their sin and he himself become the father of a great nation. But he would not have anything for himself at the cost of his people. He prayed and pleaded with God for their forgiveness. Now he goes far higher. He will sacrifice himself for them.

Try to think of him as he passes into the cloud. Listen to him as he draws near to the presence of God. Tell me his words: "Blot me, I pray Thee, out of Thy book." What book? The book of life. Not merely kill me. I think it even means: "Cast me out of Thy presence for ever and ever in this world and the world to come"! For even if the people knew little of a world to come, surely Moses knew. Did God accept his self-sacrifice? No, a mere human life could not atone for a people. But was it not grand all the same? Long afterwards another great Israelite expressed a similar wish, though he did not offer it definitely like Moses (Romans ix. 3). Who was that Israelite? Don't you think that the men who feel such things have grown very near to God? Why do you think that self-sacrifice is of the nature of God? Ah! Yes. The feeling of Moses and St. Paul was but a faint likeness of the feeling that brought the Son of God to die upon the Cross "for us men and for our salvation."

And I think it must be thus for ever. As any man grows nearer to the nature of Christ the promptings of self-sacrifice must be deeper and deeper. Even through all eternity I could never imagine that our Lord and those grown like Him would be different from that. And yet, if so, how will they bear the thought of the souls that shall be lost? It is an awful mystery. Our Lord gives us solemn, terrible warnings about the future of those who have missed of God. How one wonders about it all! Will God and those who grow like Him be satisfied about the lost? Or will the longing be there for ever to go out into the darkness, "to go after that which is lost until they find it"? How little we know! What a great deal we have yet to learn in the hereafter!

§ 2. God's Glory

That was Moses' glory, and the story leads us on now to think of God's glory, of which that of Moses was but a faint shadow. All such acts of self-sacrifice lift up the life towards God. So Moses' communion with God grew closer and deeper.

Tell me about the communion with God in the Tabernacle of the Congregation? (Notice in R.V. it is more correctly translated "The Tent of Meeting" (with God)—*see Note.*) What a deep impression it made on the people. How do you know? (xxxiii. 8). They crowded to their doors to watch as he went in, and then with awe and wonder they watched the Pillar of Cloud come and stand at the door, the visible sign of God's close communion with His servant. What a marvellous, glorious, unearthly life the man lived. How we would wish for such a life. How certain he must have always felt that God was present and attending to his prayers. How very real the unseen Spirit Life would seem to him! Could we ever expect that in our case? Perhaps not in the same degree, but surely if we are earnest in our prayers and in practising the sense of God's presence we, too, shall have much of that communion which was so dear to Moses.

But even that did not satisfy him. What more did he want? (xxxiii. 18). Hungering more and more for the Divine presence, he dared at length to desire and pray that he might see the unveiled glory of God, the beatific vision which shall be granted by-and-by to the blest in heaven. How greatly he must have loved and trusted God to dare ask that! Was this granted? Why not? (*v.* 20). It was not possible for human nature. The glory would dazzle and shrivel him up. But in some mysterious way God granted a part of his servant's desire. And God's answer is very instructive to us. Moses asked, "Show me Thy GLORY" and God said, what? "I will make all My GOODNESS pass before thee." What does that teach? Surely that *goodness* is God's glory. Tell me how God revealed His glory (xxxiv. 5-7). We cannot understand or describe it. It was not shown to Moses' bodily eye, but somehow to his soul or spirit, and the revelation was all of goodness and love. Repeat the words (*vv.* 6, 7), "The Lord God, merciful and gracious, forgiving iniquity and transgression and sin." Surely it is some hint of what we shall see and know in Heaven. Do you remember our Lord's prayer that we should get what Moses wanted? (John xvii. 24). "That they may behold My glory." What glory? Not crimson and ermine and gold and jewels, such as we imagine glory at the coronation of a king. No. What was Christ's glory on earth? The glory of Unselfishness, Self-sacrifice, Love. How glorious it seems even with all our ignorance and earthly limitations! He who took little children in His arms, who pictured God in the story of the Prodigal, of the Good Samaritan, of the Shepherd seeking His lost sheep—who died in bitter agony for His murderers and prayed as He died, "Father, forgive them." Even to our poor, stupid, earthly eyes these things seem glorious. Think what His glory by-and-by will be, which "Eye hath not seen nor ear heard, nor hath it entered into man's heart to conceive." And His children shall see that glory. We sometimes wish we had been present at some of His words and deeds on earth, as the Apostles were. Why, what is all that the Apostles ever saw to what is before us by-and-by, to behold His glory, to share in it, to be caught up into that Divine Love and Self-sacrifice till we are willing, with Moses and St. Paul, to lose, if it were possible, our very heaven itself for the sake of our brethren—willing, if such were possible, to go out into the outer darkness seeking that which is lost until we find it.

Surely it was Moses' own self-sacrifice that made him fit to be admitted after his death to God's councils in Paradise about the atonement of Christ. Why do I think he was? Yes. Because of his coming out from Paradise to the Mount of Transfiguration to talk with our Lord of "His decease which He should accomplish at Jerusalem." (Luke ix. 30, 31). Was not that a grand reward that God had for him in the Unseen Life? (See closing chapter.)

NOTES

XXXIII. 7. *The Tabernacle of the Congregation* should be "The Tent of Meeting," i.e. of meeting with God. The latter word signifies *meeting* in its most general sense, and is always used without the article before it. It does not mean a church within which the people should worship. The idea connected with it is that of Jehovah meeting with Moses or with the priests or (in only a few cases) with the people gathered into a congregation at the entrance. The English translation is not supported by the old Versions nor by the best critical authorities.

Most probably it was Moses' own tent that he thus brought out and used for this purpose till he should erect the appointed Tabernacle (see Chap. xxxv.). It was pitched "without the camp," in order that the people might feel that they had forfeited God's presence by their sin.

V. 20. Such passages show how we are to interpret the expressions "face to face" (*v.* 11), "mouth to mouth" (Numbers xii. 8).

It was vouchsafed to St. Paul as it had been to Moses to have special "visions and revelations of the Lord" (2 Corinthians xii. 1-4). He was "caught up into the third heaven and heard unspeakable words which it is not *possible* for man to utter." But he had also, like Moses, to find the narrow reach of the intellect of man in the region of Godhead. It was long after this experience in Paradise that he spoke of the Lord as "dwelling in the light which no man can approach unto, whom no man hath seen nor can see." . . . So it still remains true, "No man hath seen God at any time." (John i. 18).—*Speaker's Commentary.*

QUESTIONS FOR LESSON XIV

Recall awful sin and punishment in last lesson.

Did Moses continue angry?

How was Moses somewhat like God in his anger?

Tell the lovely thing he did for his people's sake.

How was this somewhat like what God has done for us?

Moses asked: Show me Thy glory. What was the answer? What does this teach as to the real glory of God?

⟶ God's goodness

HOW THEY BUILT
THE TABERNACLE

Read Exodus XXXV. 4 to XXXVI. 7.

See, too, Exodus XXV. 1-8.

§ 1. *"God with Us"*

We saw in the last chapter how after Moses' great act of self-sacrifice he seemed to be lifted nearer to God. He enjoyed more of the sense of God's presence. He lived in closer communion with Him. The light of God's glory shone on his face. But this sense of God's presence with them must come to all the people in proportion as each should receive it. So their next "object-lesson" was to be taught. You remember the great object-lesson in Egypt—God's POWER, God's LOVE—and then the great object-lessons of Sinai. What? God's HOLINESS. And now they are to receive their next lesson. What? (See Exodus xxv. 8.) THAT GOD WOULD DWELL AMONG THEM.

If you were Moses and had to teach this to a stupid,

137

unspiritual set of people, how do you think you would begin? A great image of God? No! you must not do that. That would be degrading to God. They had had enough of that experiment at Sinai. You must keep up the idea of God as a spirit—of God's holiness and God's majesty—and yet teach them that this great unseen Spirit, holy and majestic, was dwelling in their midst. Do you think Moses' plan of teaching it was a good one? What was it? That God should have His tent like their own. That it should stand in the midst of the encampment, that it should be taken up and set down in the journeyings just like any other—that they could come there to God and commune with Him and consult Him. And yet that though God was thus, as it were, almost as a comrade, sharing their fortunes, yet His tent must be approached only with solemnity and awe and washing and cleansing. And when one looked in there was no image nor likeness, but just a beautiful Divine supernatural light resting on the mercy seat between the wings of the cherubim. Do you think you could have discovered any better than Moses' way of teaching to stupid, ignorant slaves that the great All-holy Almighty God was dwelling in their midst? Who taught Moses this plan? God. When the world grew more fit for higher knowledge, God had another way of teaching this same lesson. How? See John i. 14, R.V., "The Word was made flesh, and TABERNACLED amongst us." That is the correct reading. God came into the midst of us as one of ourselves to be our Friend and Comrade and the sharer in our troubles.

So the Israelites were told to build a beautiful

Tabernacle with a plain tent covering it just like their own.

I wonder what they had before this. In Exodus xxxiii. 7, etc., Moses was using some sort of tent for the purpose. Perhaps some rough temporary substitute—perhaps his own tent (so the Septuagint translators put it). But, at any rate, they were now to have a brand-new Tabernacle, as beautiful and stately and dignified as it was possible for a movable tent to be. And, according to the directions they got, they must have expended a great deal of wealth on it.

§ 2. The Tabernacle

A few weeks ago I saw a very interesting effort going on in a large city parish. They were about to build a handsome new church, and the parishioners were asked to bring their offerings of money, each as he could afford, to help to build the new House of God.

Soon there was a long list of names of men and women, and a big list of children who were working for the church. One crowded infant class in the Sunday-school had resolved by their own efforts and collections to provide the new baptismal font, and all were full of interest and excitement about the undertaking before them. In a year or two I hope this new church will be completed and the people will crowd joyfully in to the dedication service to offer their gift to God.

I thought of them as I read over this chapter of Exodus. It is so like Moses wanted the Israelites, or rather God wanted them, to build their new church. Was it exactly a church for the congregation to worship in? No. We saw in the last chapter (*Note* 1) that the name "Tabernacle of the Congregation" is a mistake. It should be what? "Tent of Meeting," i.e., of meeting with God; where God's presence should be especially manifested, and where Moses could come for the people to worship and hold communion with God and receive intimations of the Divine will.

So Moses called the whole congregation together, just as the rector did in the parish I spoke of. What did he ask for? (xxxv. 5). An offering to the Lord. From whom? Every one *of a willing heart*. By whose directions did he ask it? God's. Don't you think that is exactly what should happen whenever a new church is wanted?

Of course he did not ask for money out there in the wilderness. He asked for two things. What? (1) Materials (*vv.* 5-9), (2) workmen (*v.* 10). Who were the two chief workmen who offered their skill? (*v.* 30). Tell me exactly the materials asked for in *vv.* 5, 6, 7. For this will help you to understand what they were going to make. *(Teacher should, if possible, show a picture of the Tabernacle such as shown in some of the special Teachers' Bibles.)*

There were three parts: (1) THE TABERNACLE; (2) the large goats'-hair TENT to cover and contain it; (3) the COVERING of skins to protect the tent in severe weather.

(1) The TABERNACLE was, of course, the central, the important part. It was to contain the "Ark of the

Covenant" with its two tables of stone, and was to be the place of the manifestation of the Divine Presence. It was for this Moses wanted the gold and silver and brass and onyx stones and all the beautiful cloth of blue and purple and scarlet and fine linen. Everything was to be as beautiful and dignified as could be in a movable tent.

(2) This, of course, must not stand exposed to the weather, so it was to have its TENT, large and plain and serviceable, over it. For this Moses wanted the goats'-hair cloth.

(3) Over the tent was its COVERING, the sealskin and the ramskins dyed red, laid along the roof for protection and doubtless for beauty.

For our present purpose it is not necessary to go further into detail.

§ 3. How the People Offered Willingly

What pleasant weeks passed as the people worked for their church and came out from the tents in the evening to admire each other's work and to see how much each had done, and what a pleasant sight it was that day when the people came back to Moses with their gifts!

With what interest and excitement the children would watch that crowd. The women with rolls of coloured stuffs, blue and scarlet and purple, and the shepherds with their pile of ramskins dyed red. Then the bundles of short planks of Shittim wood, and the

MOSES AND THE EXODUS

vessels of gold and silver to be melted down. And the girls coming in with their earrings and anklets and bracelets—much better than making them into a golden calf as they did last time. And the children, I wonder what they brought—their toys and gold beads and ornaments, I suppose. All these were the people "of willing heart" in the encampment. I think they were very pleased and happy that day. Why? It always makes one happy to be giving generously to any one. It must have made those "of willing heart" especially happy to be giving to God, Who had done so much for them, and Whom their nation had been treating so badly before. And I think it must have been one of the few very happy days that they gave to Moses. One wishes that the camp of Israel was always as happily employed. Soon afterwards, alas! there was a very different story to tell.

Were they content with what they brought the first day? No. Day after day the materials came in. It seemed as if they would never stop. The enthusiasm for their Tabernacle was so eager; the pleasure of giving to God was so great. At last, one day, Bezaleel and Aholiab came to Moses to tell him. What? xxxvi. 5, "The people bring more than enough, restrain them." Was it not pleasant that they had to be stopped? Do you think God was pleased? Why? Did God need their gifts? No. They were all His own that He had given them. Could God have made 1000 tabernacles with a word, without anybody helping? But He gets so little love or gratitude from human beings, that He is greatly pleased when He does get it. I heard once of a little girl who on her father's birthday got up very early to surprise him with the first pansies out of her little garden. It was pleasant to look at that father's face, he was so pleased and touched at her doing it. Yet the whole garden was his, and all that was in it had been paid for by him, even in his little girl's corner. But all the same he was so glad and pleased that she had thought of it.

I think it is like that with God, when we do anything and give anything for His service. Like those children bringing their offerings for the church that I told you of, or those who give their money to missions, or put it by for a present to brother or sister, or still better for some poor child who cannot get one otherwise, and who can make them no return. Where does our Lord say that such things are reckoned by Him as done to Himself? Matthew xxv. 40, "Inasmuch as you did it unto the least of these, ye did it unto Me." When it is so easy to give pleasure to God, what a pity we do not all try oftener to do it! Many hundreds of years later St. Paul tells us the sort of people who do this? 2 Corinthians viii. 5: "First they gave their own selves to God." Ah! if you children would all do that. "My son, give Me thine heart." (Proverbs xxiii. 26). *Teach here the duty of giving for Church support and for Missions.*

§ 4. God's Inspiration

What did Moses say he wanted besides materials? Yes, workmen. And of those who offered themselves two stood forth more important than all the rest. Who? Bezaleel and Aholiab. I daresay they were both famous artificers, each in his own line, and I daresay Moses was very glad that such splendid workers should offer themselves.

So he put them one at the head of the metal workers and engravers, the other at the head of the embroiderers and weavers. So I think of them in these days after the offerings came in, Bezaleel with his dark, swarthy workmen at the benches and the forge; Aholiab with his pale, sedentary weavers in their tents weaving at the handloom, and working on the linen their beautiful designs, and as I think of them I cannot get away from the words that God said about them. It seems to me such a lifting up and ennobling of all good work of any kind. What words? (*vv.* 31-35). Just think of it. God says, I have inspired men, filled them with My Spirit that they may be—What? Good preachers, or good authors of Scripture, or good workers of miracles? No. Good goldsmiths and clever brass workers and engravers, and cunning of hand to make beautiful embroideries, and to teach others to do it. Oh, I like that! that the Spirit of God and the interest of God is in ordinary artisans' work; that it is by His Spirit they succeed. So many people seem to think God's inspiration only belongs to the authors of Scripture, or perhaps in some minor degree to preachers of great sermons. In fact that God is not much interested in the great excellence of what is called "secular work." I read somewhere of an artist devoted to his art who turned away from religion because he was taught that, no matter how exquisitely he worked, it was not of interest to God, it was only "secular work." Is that true? Was it true of Bezaleel and

Aholiab? Do you think God cared only because it was for His Tabernacle? Surely not. I think these men when they heard these words would love God so much more and rejoice in their beautiful work, and thank God for their exquisite skill, and with glad heart dedicate it all to Him in the future.

Read

Will you try to think of it? When a fine poem or a beautiful picture moves you, or a story of adventure delights you and makes you long to be brave and faithful, that this is all through God's Spirit given to the authors of these. When you see beautiful carving or metal work or embroidery say, "It is God's gift." When you go to your own work in life by-and-by to trade or profession or business life, say, "There is nothing secular in God's sight. All true, faithful work is religious. All cleverness and deftness of hand comes from His Spirit given to me. Therefore I will think of my work as God's work. Therefore it is not merely at my prayers or my Bible-reading, or in church, but also at my ordinary work that I shall be at Divine Service."

QUESTIONS FOR LESSON XV

Show if possible a picture of the tabernacle.

What did they build the tabernacle for?

How would it keep God in their thoughts?

Tell of their eagerness in bringing materials. Show that they even brought too much.

What lesson is here for us?

Does God's Holy Spirit teach anything except religious truth?

Show here that He helps even artisans at their work.

HOW THE ISRAELITES WERE TURNED BACK FROM THE PROMISED LAND

Read Numbers III. 17 to end, XIV. 1-25,

or Deuteronomy I. v. 19 to end.

§ 1. Murmuring

We pass rapidly over the year after Sinai, and take up the journeyings again at one of the great crises in the wilderness story. Indeed, at first it must have seemed to them the end of that story. After all these weary journeys they had at last come to a time full of wonder and interest and joy and excitement. They had reached at last the goal of all their travels, the border of the Land of Promise!

Fifteen months had elapsed since they left Egypt. Do you think they were very happy months for Moses? I daresay there were some happy days in them, like those when the people gladdened his heart by offering willingly to the Lord for the Tabernacle. But I fear such

147

days were very few. In the main these were fifteen weary months of murmuring and rebellion and provoking God, and torturing the soul of the loving old chieftain who bore them as a father would bear his child in his arms, who on that memorable day in the dark clouds of Sinai had prayed, "O Lord, forgive them, and if not—blot me out of Thy book for ever!" They nearly broke his heart with their ingratitude and ill-temper, and childishness, and utter lack of any faith in God. Every difficulty frightened them as if there were no God at their backs. Every trouble made them despair and rebel and wish themselves back again in Egypt. Nothing could teach the contemptible nature of this people and the patience of God, and the love of their leader so much as this history. Do you remember some instances? What did they cry at the Red Sea when they were frightened? "Because there were no graves in Egypt hast thou taken us away to die?" (Exodus xiv. 11). In Wilderness of Sin when hungry? "Would to God we had died in the land of Egypt when we did eat bread to the full." (Exodus xvi. 3). At Rephidim when they were thirsty? "Ye have brought us out of Egypt to kill us and our children and cattle with thirst." (Exodus xvii. 3). At Sinai? "Up, make us gods," etc. (xxxii. 1). When they tired of the manna? "We remember the fish which we did eat in Egypt freely, the cucumbers, melons, leeks, etc. Now there is nothing but this manna, our soul loatheth this light bread." So it was all through the time, and so too it was, alas! in our story to-day. They could not and would not trust God, no matter what He did for them. They would murmur and doubt and rebel at everything. But this time they

148

tried it once too often, and consequences followed that the nation never forgot.

§ 2. The Hidden Future

Now try to think yourselves into the position. They were 400 miles from Egypt. They seemed reaching the end of their long journeys. The blue hills and pleasant valleys of Palestine lay in front—the land they had been hearing of since they were babies—the land that they had been looking towards all this weary time. Don't you think they would be glad and excited in those days? Do you remember the story of Columbus and his men after months of weariness and fright and danger, and their wild delight when they saw the coast line of the New World? It was like that—so delightful to have their troubles over and to come to rest out of the desert into that beautiful land flowing with milk and honey.

And don't you think it would be restful and delightful, especially to their old leader? Why? To feel that awful strain and responsibility nearly over; to rest and rule, and spend a peaceful old age with his people till the Lord should call him. Full of hope and courage, he points them to the land, "Behold, the Lord thy God hath set the land before thee: go up and possess it, as the Lord hath said; fear not, nor be discouraged." (Deuteronomy i. 21). How glad and hopeful he was about the future! How little he dreamed what was really before him! If he could look forward one short month and see what further sorrow this people would bring on him and on themselves; if he could see his forty terrible years of travel and anxiety, the sentence of exclusion and the lonely grave on Beth Peor, outside the Land which he must never enter!

He did not see it. For these few weeks at least he was hopeful and happy. Don't you think it is one of God's blessings to us that the future is hidden? Would you, if you could, lift the veil and look into your future for the next five years? Perhaps you would. We older people would not risk doing it at any price. Some of us have had big sorrows and disappointments that would have spoiled our lives if we had known of them beforehand. But we did not. We were allowed the bright, merry childhood and the hopes of our earlier life, and perhaps by the time the big sorrow came we had learned more of God and won more strength to bear it. It seems as if God were saying, "I have many things to say to you, but ye cannot bear them now." (John xvi. 12). Only One on earth was compelled to see His life beforehand— Who? And He gave wise kind advice about looking into the future—What? (Luke xii. 22, etc.) Fret not for the morrow.

§ 3. The Report of the Spies

So Moses rested peacefully in the camp at Kadesh, feeling his troubles well nigh over. What was the first step towards taking possession of the Land? Spies sent— how many? How many of them could you name? Yes, everybody remembers these two, nobody remembers the others, they did not deserve remembering.

As the camp lay still in the midnight these twelve

chiefs stole quietly up into the hills of Palestine "into the mountains," *v.* 17. How long did the host wait? Forty days. Then one day the twelve report themselves at the tent of Moses, and the whole crowd swarm round to hear the news (See Numbers xiii. 27 to xiv. 11.) What did they *all* report—(1) about the country? (2) about the inhabitants? All agreed so far. (1) Country very good; (2) People very formidable. How, then, did the two differ from the ten? Did they not think the inhabitants strong? But what? They thought God was stronger— that's all. The ten looked at the difficulties and thought little about God. The two looked at God and thought little about the difficulties. What does Scripture call this latter attribute? Faith. How did the people receive the report of the ten spies? What did they murmur? (xiv. 3).

What a striking scene! The angry, terrified, disappointed crowd listening first to the ten faithless princes who forgot that God was with them, and timidly calculated the chances of conquering—and then refusing to hear the other two as they rose to speak amid howls and curses, beseeching the people to be men, to trust God, to go forward fearlessly in His strength. Then Moses tries to quiet them. It is not told in Numbers, but it is pathetic to hear the old man himself, long years afterwards, telling it. "I said to you, Dread not, nor be afraid, for the Lord your God shall fight for you, according to all that He did in Egypt before your eyes." (Deuteronomy i. 29, 30). Would they listen to him? *v.* 4, to depose him from his leadership, to make a new chief. Ay, they did more than propose, they did appoint the new leader instead of him. How do we know? (See Nehemiah ix. 17.) I think Moses must have felt that sorely. This was the people for whom his whole life had been given up since that far-back day in Egypt when "it came into his heart" to visit his brethren the children of Israel, for whom he prayed, "If Thou will not forgive them, blot me out of Thy book." This is the return for it.

Again Caleb and Joshua join him in the pleading, *vv.* 6-9. Was it any use? They got so angry that they actually wanted to—what? (*v.* 10) stone them! What saved them? Ah! suddenly a bright light flashing through the cloudy pillar startled them all. God was looking! God was listening all the time! Ah! they were quiet enough now. That awful vision had effectually frightened them.

§ 4. *The Punishment and Its Lesson*

What is God's complaint of them? *v.* 11. Their obstinate, hopeless unbelief, "They will not believe for all the signs I have showed among them." What could be done with such a people? Did Moses plead for them? Tell of the exquisite plea he used, *vv.* 17, 18. Where had he learned that? Ah! you remember, that day when God showed him His glory (Exodus xxxiii. 19). "I beseech Thee, according as Thou hast spoken, saying the Lord is long suffering and of great mercy, forgiving iniquity and transgression, etc. Pardon, I beseech Thee, the iniquity of this people as Thou hast done from Egypt until now."

Were they forgiven? Partly. But a very severe sentence was pronounced. What? (*vv.* 29, 30, 33). Did they deserve it? Remember their prayer (*v.* 2), "Would to God we had died in the wilderness." It was terribly answered. Yes, said God, you shall die in the wilderness: "To-morrow turn you, and get you back into the wilderness by the way of the Red Sea." If hasty, passionate wishes were often answered as literally, people would be more careful in wishing.

Why could they not enter into the Land after two years instead of forty years? Because not fit. See what Apostle said 1000 years after (Hebrews iii. 19). They could not enter in because of unbelief. If they had got into Palestine in that condition of mind, with no faith, no discipline, no deep care for the religious life, they would have fallen in a few years to the level of the Canaanites, and God's great purpose for the world would have been spoiled.

So you see they had to wait forty years for what they might have had in one year. Does it not seem a stupid waste of happiness?

I think there is a lesson for young people here. There is a beautiful, restful life that Christ promises here on earth. "Come unto Me, and I will give you rest." All who live for Christ are happier and more restful than others. Often people worry and struggle for many years of a worldly, godless life, and at last, in the end, weary and heavy laden, come to Christ for rest. *But what a pity they did not come earlier.* The Rest was waiting, but they were not ready. They might have

153

come in childhood as many others did. They did not believe in the happiness of religion, or they thought it was too hard to be religious. And so they lost much of life's rest and happiness. Is it not a little bit like the Israelites who could have entered the Land after about a year, but "entered not in because of unbelief"?

§ 5. *Moses' Disappointment and Its Lesson*

But was not Moses disappointed too, though he did not deserve it? Yes. God has often to disappoint us for other reasons than punishment. It must have been a terrible disappointment. All the strain and responsibility and worry and torment of that people put back on him for forty years. Are we told how he bore it? No. But we can guess. Surely there was no rebellious feeling, however hard it was. The brave, loyal heart bowed to God's will and went out again to the dreary desert. I think, after all his close communion with God, he must have felt sure that God's will was the best thing for him and for them all—that God had more work for him before he entered into his final rest. That was comfort enough for Moses. Hard, bitter things come to many in this life, but it is one thing to have to bear them as punishment for our wrong-doing, as in the Jews' case here, and quite another when they come in the path of duty and are taken up bravely for the love of God, as in Moses' case.

NOTES

Ch. xiii. 1, *The Lord spake*, etc., does not contradict Deuteronomy i. 22, which says that the suggestion came from the people and pleased Moses. Moses would surely seek God's guidance. Quite possibly the suggestion to send spies arose from their own unbelief, and that it was only *permitted*, not enjoined, by God.

V. 6, Caleb is repeatedly called "the Kenezite." (Chap. xxxii. 12; Joshua xiv. 6, 14). Some think, therefore, that he was a Canaanite (Genesis xv. 19) received into the nation of Israel. It is interesting to think of Joshua and Caleb long years afterwards talking over this incident of the spies when they were both old men, one of them the commander-in-chief of Israel, the other seemingly still a simple soldier of fortune (Joshua xiv. 6, etc.).

V. 16, *Oshea, Jehoshua.* The original name means help or salvation. The new name adds on as a prefix the contraction of Jehovah's name, i.e. *"Jehovah is the help."* If Moses gave him his new name now, it would be quite natural, in relating the history afterwards, to use this new name as in Exodus.

V. 20, Time of "first grapes," i.e. about our month of August.

V. 22, *Before Zoan in Egypt.* How natural to think of their old city in Egypt. It is thought that Hebron and the original foundation of Tanis were both Hittite. See Lesson I.

Vv. 22, 28. Children of Anak, i.e. of the Anakim, the giants.

QUESTIONS FOR LESSON XVI

Who were Caleb and Joshua?

Had the Israelites to wait forty years before reaching Palestine?

How soon did they reach the border? Why not go in?

Tell of the spies and their report.

How did the people behave?

Tell of other cases where they behaved thus.

What was their punishment now?

LESSON XVII

KORAH, DATHAN AND ABIRAM

Read Numbers XVI.

§ 1. Causes of the Rebellion

We have read of the stern punishment on Israelites for their rebellion at Kadesh. What punishment? Now, do you think they were sorry or penitent? I don't, and I think this story to-day shows it. I think they were like sullen children punished for a fault, who were afraid to do more than sulk in silence with black looks and angry hearts. They were angry at Moses and Aaron, and, I suppose, at Joshua and Caleb. I'm afraid, even at God. At least a great number were. Are boys and girls sometimes like that when punished? And it was this sullen anger that gave opportunity for the other evil passions that found vent in this rebellion of Korah.

Let us see if we can understand this rebellion. What two tribes engaged in it? Why these two, do you think? The men of Levi were proud and elated at the recent praise given them for their action about Golden Calf.

157

What action? And proud also that they were specially called to be the clergy of the nation. And Reuben? Remember Reuben was the eldest son, and probably the Reubenite men were very jealous that he had lost his birthright, and that their tribe had not got chief place and had to yield to Judah. There is also an interesting reason why these two tribes would be likely to join in conspiracy. What? Not easy to find it, but see Numbers ii. 16, 17, and Numbers x. 18-21 (Kohathites). These two tribes always marched next each other.

So the first thing we see is that the cause of the rebellion was the evil passions of the conspirators— Selfishness, Presumption, Sullenness, Discontent. Instead of taking God's rebuke humbly and trying to be good and yielding to God's law for the government of the camp, they began to think about themselves and their grievances, and that they had been hardly treated—that they were just as good as any one else—or better—and that their neighbours did not set on them at all the high value which they deserved. Did you ever feel like that? I suppose Korah wanted to be high priest himself instead of Aaron, and that Dathan and Abiram thought they could rule better than Moses. And I dare say the 250 princes thought they were fit for higher positions and greater distinctions. In most cases I should hesitate to assume these evil motives. It is wrong to do so without reason. We should be slow in judging men's motives. But when I see the attitude of these men who knew all about God's laws and God's appointing of Moses and Aaron, I cannot attribute to them any higher motives than these. So they began to grow disobedient and insolent and troublesome in the camp. And for some time before the outbreak Moses could notice the black looks and the scoffing taunts and the grumbling, forced obedience to his orders. And this thing grew and grew till it became upsetting to all discipline and dangerous to the whole camp. The Reubenites would not see why Moses, who did not belong to the tribe of the eldest son, should rule them. The Levites would not see why Aaron, who was but a Levite like themselves, should be at their head. "Why should these two brothers usurp authority over Israel? Are not we just as good as they? Are not all the Lord's people holy as well as they?" So they talked. A nice lot *they* were to talk of being holy, with all their past and their present conduct! I suppose they referred to God's speaking of the whole nation as a "holy nation" (Exodus xix. 6). But see there what God said should make them a holy nation. What? Were they doing that? Very far from it. Thus the rebellion grew and grew underground without open rupture. But at last it reached great dimensions. How great? (See *v.* 2.) When 250 princes and leaders were in it, it certainly was a serious matter. But I suspect it was even worse than it looks. In *vv.* 24, 27, I read of the "Tabernacle" of Korah, Dathan, and Abiram, and the Hebrew word is that commonly used of the Tabernacle of the Congregation (see notes). Quite possibly they had dared to set up a rival Tabernacle!

§ 2. Its Wickedness and Danger

Now try if you can see exactly (1) the wickedness,

(2) the danger of this rebellion. 1st.—Why was it so wicked? Because Moses and Aaron had *not* usurped or taken to themselves their authority. Who had appointed them? God Himself, who also appointed these other Levites to serve Him in their lower positions, and these Reubenites and these 250 princes each to the duties allotted to him. You see God was really their King, and the people knew it very well, and knew that all the offices in the nation were the different ways of serving God. Therefore, their rebellion, as Moses told them, was not against him, but against God's arrangements (*vv.* 28-31).

Suppose in the American army and navy two brothers were appointed Commander-in-Chief and Admiral. Suppose 250 army and navy officers began to be mutinous and mock at their authority, and say, "We are just as good as you and we know as much, and we have as good a right to be chiefs and we will not obey you." What do you think they would reply? "You may be as good and as wise and as clever as we, but the President has put us in these positions, and we must uphold them at any risk. It is his affair. Go and complain to him if you like, and tell him how foolish he was to appoint us. But meantime obey orders, or take the consequences." What do you think the President and the Government would do to these rebels if they persisted? It would be clearly a rebelling, not against those chiefs, but against the President and would be terribly punished. So you see the wickedness of the attitude of Korah's company—rebellion against God.

But now see the grave *danger* of it. Suppose these

American officers thus to mutiny, what would become of rule and discipline in the army and navy? It would be destroyed, and America would be at the mercy of any invader. Ought the Government allow such danger to exist? But suppose this should occur when a foreign army was invading America, and that there were hostile forces all around ready to spring on our army at the first chance, what would become then of the mutinous officers? A short shrift indeed. I think the commander-in-chief would march them all out some fine morning, with a blank wall behind them and files of soldiers ready in front to shoot them down at a moment when the word was given. Would that be wrong or cruel? Would it not be better to shoot 250 obstinate rebels than to risk the ruin of the whole nation?

Now this was the position in Israel. If the firm hand of authority and discipline was once removed, these two millions of people would become not a nation but a mob, free to do what they liked, ready to fly at each other's throats, and so there would be an end of God's plans for Israel. And besides this, all around them were fierce tribes of Amalekites and Midianites waiting to spring on them at any opportunity. So you can easily see the seriousness of this outbreak.

§ 3. The Challenge of Moses

Now let us follow the story. Picture this formidable procession with 250 famous princes and men of renown marching to Moses' tent, and a great crowd watching behind, half-frightened, half-sympathetic. Moses comes out of his tent to listen to their complaints. Not a very pleasant people to have to listen to. Insolent and insubordinate, they challenge him to his teeth. "Ye take too much upon you, ye sons of Levi." What is their charge against Moses and Aaron? (*v.* 3). Does Moses vindicate or defend himself? (*vv.* 4, 5). No. He falls on his face in prayer and then leaves it to God to vindicate him. "To-morrow God will show who are His and who is holy."

Fancy any one thinking Moses was self-seeking and usurping authority for his own purposes! He who had prayed for them—"God forgive the people, and if not, blot me out of Thy book." It must have hurt him deeply. Yet he was sure God would not think it or misunderstand him, and that contented him. So it should be with us when falsely charged. God knows. Christ will not misunderstand.

Show how he pointed out that God had given to these men their duties as He had given Moses his, and that their rebellion was against God, not against him and Aaron. I think he wanted to get the whole body of the conspirators together to discuss things with them. He had only Korah and his friends present, so he sent orders to the other princes, Dathan and Abiram, to attend. What was their reply? Flat disobedience, and insult added to it (*vv.* 12-15). No discipline could be kept up, no camp could hold together if the commander were to be thus treated. So there was nothing for it but to fling down his challenge to the rebels and call upon God to vindicate his position. "Be thou and all thy company before the Lord," he says to Korah, "thou, and they, and Aaron, to-morrow. To-morrow the Lord shall judge between us."

§ 4. *How God Judged the Rebels*

The morrow is come. The great Testing Day to tell if Moses or the rebels shall be supreme in the nation. Make in your minds the picture that I see. The huge camp of Israel stretching along the hillside. In the midst of it I see a great open space, an open valley crowded with thousands and thousands of excited people, gazing eagerly up the slope before them. Gaze up with them. There, on the south side of the Tabernacle, is the camp of Reuben, marked by the standards of the tribe, and in the front of it the two white princes' tents of Dathan and Abiram. In front to the right I see the tall tent of Moses, and opposite it, in the open, the coloured curtains of the Tabernacle, with the sun blazing brightly on its roof of scarlet ramskins. Something else, too, the sun is blazing on. A crowd of men in white in the front of the Tabernacle, holding in their hands what seem bright brazen shields. You know these. Korah and his company of white-robed Levites, carrying their brazen censers.

That is the picture on which the host of people is gazing. They are wrought to a high pitch of excitement and suspense. What is going to happen? Moses has challenged the test of a miracle. He has appealed to Jehovah. The rebels have responded by standing daringly in their places. Now what would happen next?

I wonder if Moses had any doubt about the result. I don't think he had. Keep your eyes still on the hillside in front. I see the old chief come forth from his tent, and the people almost cease breathing in their suspense. Dathan and Abiram have not stood forward with Korah. They are standing sullenly at the door of their tents, with a crowd of followers round them. But they are not to escape thus. Straight to the rebel tents the leader walks, and warns their half-frightened followers to withdraw. Then, after his stern glance has swept over Reubenites and Levites, he turns solemnly to the crowd below. "If these men die the common death of all men, then the Lord hath not sent me." The faces of the crowd are white with excitement. For a moment there is a great solemn, awful hush—then a rumbling as of thunder—a rocking and quaking of the ground—a wild shrieking of terror—a flash of white blinding light from the Tabernacle, and lo! when the people could look again, the whole ground on the hill slope had cleft asunder and swallowed the two white tents, and across in the open the men with the brazen censers lay charred and dead upon the ground, blasted by that quick flash from the Tabernacle behind them!

§ 5. Lessons

1. Are some of you troubled about the wives and little children swallowed up with the obstinate rebels in their ruin? Do you think it seemed a bit hard on them? Don't be afraid to think out fearlessly about it. Be very reverent and humble in judging. But don't be afraid to think and inquire. It is probably the conscience and the tenderness that God has given you, and the belief you

have as to what God would do, that is prompting such thoughts. At any rate, they are better spoken out than kept in. I do not know enough to answer your thoughts. But I know enough to keep myself undisturbed. I know that God is more merciful than I am—that these women and children had not passed to their final destiny, but only to the great Waiting Life beyond the grave, where they are as much in God's sight and in God's care as they were here. Why should we be afraid to trust them with God? "Shall not the Judge of all the earth do right?" Aye and more than right for them and for all.

2. Take care lest you fall into the spirit of such sins—sullenness, self-seeking, discontent, thinking yourself better than those in higher positions than yourself, and wishing to discredit them and make little of them. There are two ways of trying to get equal with those above us—(1) trying to pull them down; (2) a nobler way, trying to rouse ourselves up. But there is a nobler way still—Thinking more about your work than your position. Letting God settle your position for you, and "doing your duty in that state of life unto which it shall please God to call you."

3. There is another lesson that needs in our day to be taught very distinctly, and yet very cautiously, lest it should be wrongly taught. God forbid that there should be self-conceit or arrogance between one body of Christians and another. But we must not blink plain facts where our Lord's interests are concerned. Just as in the old Jewish days, when God called a nation to accomplish great purposes, so in our day. Our Lord certainly appointed a visible Church on earth to

accomplish a great purpose. The chief work of His life was the training of its leaders and starting it on its course. He certainly willed that it should remain one and unbroken. It has not done so. It is not our place to apportion the blame. Sometimes it was some of the truest, noblest souls that in their perplexity made divisions, thinking it was their duty. Sometimes the evil came from men's self-will and their failure to understand each other. It is not for us to judge. But we must see the evil, and see the weakness caused by this setting up of rival "Tabernacles of God" through the land. Try to sympathise and join in the efforts of holy men of all denominations who are trying to put this evil right—that our Lord's great prayer may be fulfilled, "That they all may be one," (i.e. outwardly one as well as inwardly, for He adds) "that *the World may know* that Thou hast sent Me." (John xvii. 21).

NOTES

V. 1, Korah, son of Izhar, brother of Amram, was Moses' and Aaron's relative, and was evidently jealous of the position which they had received. On is not mentioned again—perhaps he withdrew from the conspiracy before the catastrophe.

V. 14, *Wilt thou put out the eyes?* i.e. "Are you trying to blind us to what you are doing?"

Vv. 19, 21, "All the congregation." This shows how the mutiny had grown, and that the people were largely sharing in its spirit.

Vv. 24, 27, Tabernacle: the Hebrew word is *mishkan*, and usually denotes the Tabernacle, i.e. the inner Tabernacle under its tent. It may possibly only mean the tent or dwellings of Korah, Dathan, and Abiram (see *v.* 26). But some commentators think it means a rival Tabernacle set up by the rebels.

V. 32. It would seem that Korah was not with Dathan and Abiram, but probably was destroyed with the men burned up at the Tabernacle door. This is further probable from the statement in ch. xxvi. 11. Here we learn that Korah's children "died not" like those of Dathan and Abiram (see also Psalms cvi. 17).

QUESTIONS FOR LESSON XVII

Who said, "Ye take too much upon you, ye sons of Levi"?

Who were Korah, Dathan and Abiram?

What was the cause of their rebellion?

Show the danger of such a rebellion, say, in the American army.

How did Moses meet them?

What was their punishment?

If some one said that God was cruel in letting these families also be destroyed, could you say anything in reply?

LESSON XVIII

HOW MOSES SINNED AND SUFFERED

Read Numbers XX. 1-13.

Deuteronomy XXXII. 51.

Psalms CVI. 33.

§ 1. Back Again at Kadesh

We have to do to-day what is generally an unsatisfactory thing in the story of a man's life—skip over thirty-eight years of it in silence. We have had to do it before—when? The whole of his life in Midian. Why? We had no information about it. So here. We have a long list of the camping-places during the desert wanderings (see Numbers xxxiii.), but with few exceptions the names are lost in obscurity and have very little of interest recorded.

From the silence of Scripture I think this period is intended to be a blank. All that happened in these thirty-eight years of God's strange discipline and

168

training of Israel is hidden from us. It looks as if it had been a dull, monotonous time for them, since so little of interest is recorded. I suppose they often lay for months or perhaps years without change. But it had done them good—great good. In spite of the sad story of to-day, this people who have come back to the borders of the Promised Land are clearly a better people. Were these the same people who were turned back into the wilderness? No (xiv. 28-30). Their carcasses had fallen in the wilderness. These were the boys and girls of that day now grown to be men and women, a new and better race after all these years of training in God's presence continually. I don't think the old race was entirely gone yet (see Deuteronomy ii. 14, 16). I think some of the bad ones remained, and perhaps that partly accounts for the murmuring and rebellion again now.

So the forty years of desert journey are nearly over at last. We are drawing towards the close of the story of Moses. We have a very sad part of it to-day. It tells of the only sin that has been recorded for us of him whom we have so learned to admire and love all through this history. Now, first of all, be clear about the place. Where had they come to? (*v.* 1). Kadesh. Where was that? When were they last there? (Numbers xiii. 26). What happened there? Yes. Kadesh was that place on the border of Palestine, where thirty-eight years ago they had been brought to see the land and enter it, where they sent out the spies, and from which through their wicked rebellion they were turned back into the wilderness to wander for all these years.

Back again at Kadesh. And Moses is sad for a family

169

trouble—what? Miriam is dying—or dead; she died at Kadesh. Should not you think that would solemnize the people a little? What else should have done so? The awful memory of the Korah rebellions (*v.* 3), and I think the old memories of what happened on that same spot thirty-eight years ago. But it did not. What was the trouble now? That huge host with their cattle were too much for the waters of Kadesh—drought came, and great anxiety. Then what happened? Yes. One would think these thirty-eight years were but a bad dream, and that we were back again in the old Kadesh days, so exactly was the scene of the old rebellion reproduced. "Would to God we had died with our brethren in Korah's rebellion! Wherefore have ye brought us up out of Egypt into this evil place?" Had they ever before been in like plight? (Exodus xvii.). And had God delivered them and kept them supplied for forty years? Do you think you would have been so patient with them?

What did Moses and Aaron do? Fell on their faces in prayer and intercession at the door of the Tent of Meeting where God's presence was specially shown. That was Moses' one resort in every trouble and anxiety. He went to God always. Don't you think he and Aaron were frightened? Well they might be. Here they were on the very place where thirty-eight years ago they had all been turned back. Were they to repeat it all again, to lose the land again, to be sent forth once more into that terrible wilderness till another generation died? No wonder they were frightened. What was the result of their prayer? What did God direct?

§ 2. Smiting the Rock

Now the rest of this story puzzles me. I have formed such a high opinion of Moses that I can't understand how he could fail so badly here, after having behaved so grandly in far more difficult times. I should have thought that his old habit of falling on his face before God, and bringing all his troubles and perplexities to Him, would be enough for him. That he would leave his troubles and vexations there with God, and come forth strong and peaceful as at other times to do the best in the crisis before him. But evidently he did not, nor Aaron either. They did what many people do still, carry troubles and vexations to God in prayer, and then carry them away with them again to fret over.

Should not you have thought, too, that he would be glad that God was so kind and merciful, and gone forth with glad heart to do his commission? Ordinary people might be different, but we expect such great things from Moses.

Next day we have another of these magnificent pictures in the history of Israel. (I wish some great artist would paint them, as Tissot and Doré have done in the "Life of Christ.") The vast host of Israel in their hundreds of thousands assembled in front of the great cliff of Kadesh—the rocks bare and dry, the grass brown and burnt up, the men and women and little children tortured with the heat and thirst, waiting for the miracle. And then at last Aaron comes in his beautiful robes, and Moses is beside him. But instead of the calm dignity of the high priest and the face of the old leader shining with

171

God's presence, there is a change—a look of hesitancy and doubt and angry irritation. And the people stand wondering to see their chieftain, who has been for forty years their example of all good, come forth angry and petulant, and fiercely strike the rock twice with his rod without even speaking to it at all as directed, and turn fiercely to the waiting crowd. "Ye rebels must we" (or rather, *Can* we) "fetch you water out of this rock?"

Whatever Moses' fault, did it prevent God's mercy to the people? Immediately a great torrent of cool, clear water burst from the rock, and the people shouted exultingly as they rushed forward to drink. But do you think there was much exulting in the heart of the old chief? Ah! he knew what he had done, that he had grieved and dishonoured God and shattered his own peace and his own future by these two strokes on the rock. For the Lord said—what? "Because ye believed Me not, to sanctify Me in the eyes of the children of Israel, therefore ye shall not bring this congregation into the land which I have given them."

§ 3. Moses' Sin

Ah, poor old leader! in the anger and unbelief of a moment he had spoiled his life. Are you thinking in your heart, though you don't like to say it, that God was a little bit hard on him for this one sin? Best that you should learn to express candidly though very humbly and reverently about such thoughts. It is probably because you have so high a belief about God that you think He could not be unfairly hard on any one. Besides, in asking such questions you are more likely to find the answer.

Now what do you really think Moses' sin was? I am not at all sure myself. I am told that it was that he was angry, or that he struck the rock twice, or that he said, "Must *we* fetch you water?" giving glory to himself, or that what he really said was, "*Can* we fetch you water?" (see notes), showing unbelief in God. Verse 12 gives some colour to this latter opinion. They are all bad sins. Probably his sin was made up of all of them together. But I think there was something worse since the loving, patient God punished so severely such a loving, faithful, devoted servant as Moses. We have only a very brief, condensed account. I think if we knew all, we should see some serious aggravation of the fault that does not appear to us. In some way, too, it was necessary *for the people's sake* that Moses should not escape severe punishment for his sin (see Deuteronomy i. 27; iv. 21). "The Lord was angry with me for your sake." We know that it was a sin of unbelief and of dishonouring God. We know that it must have been of a very serious nature to call for such a punishment. Beyond that we can only guess in what it exactly consisted.

But it spoiled and saddened his last days. To feel he had dishonoured God would be sorer pain to Moses than any punishment God might inflict. It is the only blot in his glorious career, and it is a warning to us all. "Let him that thinketh he standeth, take heed lest he fall." If even so noble a soul as Moses could fall into such a serious sin, how watchful we should be! There was only One who ever walked on earth on whom the devil had no power. "The Prince of this World cometh, and hath nothing in Me."

I have often wondered how it was that he fell. For some time past something must, I think, have been going wrong with him. A grave slip like that does not usually come in a moment and without previous smaller slips in preparation. I wonder had he been keeping up his communion with God? That was always his great strength. It is the great strength of every man who practises it. The quiet little time in the morning and evening and at all other hours, of prayer and meditation and "talking to God" and reading one's Bible—and our public worship, especially Holy Communion. These are life's great strength, and when they are neglected there is danger of a fall. I don't like to suspect Moses of this even for a short time. But it may have been. Perhaps the weary, monotonous wanderings in the desert had tired his soul out. Perhaps he was troubled and vexed at Miriam's illness and death. And perhaps—but this is a mere guess. I see a curious statement in *ch.* xii. 1 about him. What? Miriam was angry with him about an Ethiopian woman whom he had married. I wonder could it mean that Zipporah was dead, and that he had married again, a stranger outside of Israel? And if sc, I wonder if this Ethiopian wife was of a lower type and dragged down his high thoughts and ideals, and so life was not kept at its old high level. I don't know. This is all guessing. But I feel that something had been probably going wrong for some time. It was only a great *slip*, not a permanent *fall*. And I am sure his great sorrow helped him to recover himself soon. But it was a slip, a bad slip.

§ 4. Lessons

(1) What do you think are the two chief lessons of this? You easily guess the first. Don't neglect your daily prayers and Bible-reading. Don't let them grow cold or careless, else your life will drop lower, and the bad slips will come.

(2) And I think we learn another lesson. Do you think God forgave Moses in his great sorrow? And loved him still? Yes. I think it teaches us the loving sternness of God that can forgive a man and love him and yet insist on letting the punishment of his sin come on him for his good. When you come to the story of his death I think you will see that the punishment was not really much of punishment at all, since God was taking him to a far nobler and lovelier Promised Land. I am sure Moses would see it in that light afterwards. But don't you think while here on earth that he felt the punishment sorely? I feel touched as I see how he longed for that land, how longingly he speaks afterwards in Deuteronomy; that good land, he says, that land of rivers and fountains—the land of wheat and barley—of vines and pomegranates and figs, the land of oil olives and honey. Nobody could guess from this quiet, reserved history in the Book of Numbers what a longing was in the old man's heart. But it nearly brings tears into one's eyes to see him exposing his heart's desire in his farewell speech in Deuteronomy,

and we find that he whose pleadings had nearly always been for others, had in secret pleaded eagerly to God for himself. "I besought God, Let me go over, I pray Thee, and see the good land that is beyond Jordan, that goodly mountain, and Lebanon. But the Lord said to me, "Let it suffice thee. Speak to Me no more on this matter." (Deuteronomy iii. 23-26). Does it not all show how sorely he felt it?

Some people cannot understand how punishment should be possible along with God's pardon and love, just because of their wretched vulgarizing of the ideas connected with God's chastisement. To get rid of the penalty is their one idea of being forgiven. To the true servant of God it is not the penalty that matters so much, but the fact that God is "out with him," as children say, "not friends with him." I saw one day a child ordered to bed for the day for some wrong-doing. He had been warned that that punishment would be the result if he committed that fault. By-and-by the little chap expressed his sorrow and his mother forgave him and kissed him. Do you think she should then have let him get up? Even though she had warned and threatened that punishment beforehand? I am quite sure she should not. At any rate, being a wise mother, she did not, and the boy quite understood that his penalty must remain. But it did not matter much then. It was easy to bear it since mother was "friends with him" again and had kissed him.

So it was with Moses. The Lord forgave His beloved servant. But the temporal consequences of his sin must remain. So it was with David, "The Lord also hath put away thy sin. Howbeit the child shall die." (2 Samuel xii. 13, 14). So it is with us. For our worst sins there is plenteous redemption. Our sins may become white as snow and pass away altogether so far as saddening or disturbing our relations with God. Yet that sin may keep on its punishment for years afterwards—may leave in our lives—in our characters, in our reputation, in our health, in our position, in a hundred different ways may leave its traces and consequences; e.g. a liar or a drunkard or a dishonest or dishonourable man; the results will remain after he has repented and been forgiven and is struggling nobly, comforted by the love of God. God will not take away the results. But like the mother who kissed and forgave and restored her love to her boy, He will bless them to us and make them easy to bear.

So Moses had to look forward in his closing days to putting aside all his proud ambitions for Israel and dying in the wilderness and letting another lead them in. But God was with him and comforted him. So he could bear it.

NOTES

V. 1, Abode in Kadesh. Some people think that Kadesh remained a sort of headquarters all the forty years, though the tribes were scattered about through the wilderness. They certainly abode a good while there, "many days," Moses says, Deuteronomy i. 46.

V. 3, This is evidently a reference to Korah's rebellion.

177

But it seems puzzling. Why should this be so prominent in their minds if it were thirty-eight years ago? And in v. 4 it does not look natural that after forty years they should be still asking, "Why have ye brought us up out of Egypt?" One might reply that the case of Korah was so terrible that the older people could never forget it—and that the words "Why have ye brought us up" should be rather "Why did ye bring us up out of Egypt at all?" Probably that is the explanation. But it is hard to feel sure about the exact order of the events and the intervals between them.

V. 10, Must we fetch, etc. What did Moses really say? What was his sin? Did he say, "Must *we* fetch," etc., taking God's honour to himself? If the *we* were thus emphatic the personal pronoun would probably have occurred in the Hebrew for emphasis. But it does not. From the references to it afterwards it would seem more probable that Moses and Aaron were somewhat distrustful of God's promise and His power: *"Can* we fetch you water," etc.

QUESTIONS FOR LESSON XVIII

The Israelites are again at Kadesh on the Palestine border. When had they been there before? What had happened there?

How many years since then?

What family sorrow fell on Moses at Kadesh? What earlier mention have we of Miriam?

Now tell of the one recorded sin of Moses' life.

It must have been worse than it seems for it brought a severe punishment. What?

Yet surely God forgave and loved Moses though he punished him. Can you explain how pardon and punishment could go together?

LESSON XIX

BALAAM—A STUDY OF CONSCIENCE, PART I

Read Numbers XXII.

Micah VI. 5-8.

These two lessons on Balaam require a great deal of study by the teacher, and careful preparation to condense them into required time.

§ 1. Conscience

After Moses had sinned, and been sentenced to exclusion from the Land, he went on still, like a brave man, to do his duties just as if no sorrow had fallen on him at all. He led on his people nearer to Palestine, and in so doing had to fight with Sihon, king of the Amorites, and Og, the giant king of Bashan. At last he approaches the borders of Moab.

And here comes in one of the most interesting incidents in the whole history—the story of the King of Moab and the prophet Balaam. I wonder if Moses knew anything about it at the time? Indeed, I wonder how he ever came to know of it? There are parts of it that no one but Balaam could have told. I have sometimes thought that perhaps Balaam, when expelled in disgrace from the Moabite camp for refusing to curse Israel, may have come to the Israelite encampment, and told Moses, or told somebody. Or perhaps the Balaam story remained as a separate story, and only got used up afterwards in the composition of the Pentateuch. Many people, you know, think that Moses did not complete the whole Pentateuch as we have it, but only left the documents which were the foundation or kernel from which it was afterwards written in the finished form as we have it to-day. We do not really know.

But at any rate here is a most wonderful and most interesting story. Also, in some ways, a difficult story. It will require your hardest thinking and deepest attention. But I don't think it is too hard for you if you do your best. And if you can understand it, it will be for you full of interest and instruction.

Before we talk of it, I want to ask you some questions. Have you ever shut your eyes and turned your thoughts in on your conscience—the part of you where God's Holy Spirit dwells, and through which He speaks to you? Ever felt it saying within you, "You ought," "You ought not," when you were thinking of doing something? Who put it in you? Why? As a guide like the Pillar of cloud. But if it is your guide, what do we want Bible for? To teach about God. To educate and enlighten the conscience, which is only given to us in a weak, imperfect, uneducated stage. We have to educate and enlighten it. The Bible does that. It can guide us a little even without the Bible or Christian teaching. But not much.

You have felt conscience saying, "You ought," "You ought not." Now, if, when conscience says, "You ought," you reply, "I will not," what happens? Do you remember? Does conscience begin to hurt you, and accuse you, and drag you up before its bar and judge you? Did you ever feel that? And sometimes in the night, when you have been bad, have you felt conscience frightening you, and pointing out into the Unseen World, to tell of Someone behind who is noticing your badness? I want you to get the habit of watching and studying that conscience in yourselves, the most wonderful and interesting study. It makes one solemn and serious, for it is the voice of God in us. Through it the Holy Spirit speaks.

Now this story is in the Bible, like all its other stories, to educate and enlighten our conscience. But this has in it a special warning. It tells of a man who played tricks with his conscience instead of obeying it, and shows the great danger of doing this.

For example. Here is a clear duty lying before you. What does conscience say? "You ought." But you greatly dislike doing it. So you may bluntly say, "I will not," and thus openly disobey, or you may try to play tricks with conscience, and persuade yourself that conscience is not saying that, or that there are special reasons in your case which make your refusal not real wrong-doing, etc. This latter is the sort of thing that Balaam did, and this story is to warn us against it.

§ 2. Balaam

How does Balaam come into the Israelites' story? Yes; heathen people have great belief in magic and in cursing enemies. We had instances in India where the natives brought their heathen prophets and magicians to curse British troops. Don't you think Balaam a very remarkable man? Why? (1) He was a man of great fame and reputation, whom powerful kings far away would send for to help them. (2) He seems to have been a teacher and prophet of God, in some degree like Moses himself, though very different in character. Read his wonderful words in Micah (vi. 5-8), "What doth the Lord require of thee," etc. (3) More remarkable still, he was a prophet of God in the midst of heathen people, outside the Jewish race.

What does that teach us? That God's care and teaching was not confined to Israel, though He was specially training Israel as a teacher of the world. You remember the other instances before? Melchizedek in Canaan, Job in Arabia, Jethro in Midian, Jonah in Nineveh, etc. So even in China and India the false religions of to-day are corruptions of higher, nobler teaching of long ago, and all high, noble teaching must come from God. So we find God was not neglecting all the rest of the world for Israel. Balaam seems to have come from Abraham's native land in Mesopotamia. Perhaps some knowledge of God had remained through Abraham's family.

Balaam, then, was no mere magician or juggler, but

a man called by God to very high things, who spoiled all his life through playing tricks with his conscience.

What specially concerns us, then, is his character. Not merely because he was a man of high religious *belief* (such as expressed in Micah vi. 8), sinking to shameful *conduct*, but also that he was able to deceive himself and persuade himself that he was not opposing God, when all the time he was moving fast towards one of the most horrible crimes in history. His is a very mournful story, one of the many mournful stories in the world—of men called to high things who have chosen low, of men who through their own evil and self-deceiving have wrecked their lives.

§ 3. Playing Tricks with Conscience

Now for the story. The great prophet is one day in his tent in far Mesopotamia, when a procession arrives of chieftains and princes of Moab, with their tall, lumbering camels and their gaudy, barbaric trappings. Who sent them? What for? How did he receive their message? Then he inquired of God, and learned God's will, perhaps in a dream, perhaps as Moses learned it. I don't know how. What did he reply to the messengers? (*v.* 13). Was not that a perfectly right answer? Do you see anything doubtful or suspicious in it? Does he say out straight, "God's will is my will, I will not go"? No. What? "The Lord *refuseth to give me leave.*" Does it not suggest that he wished God would give him leave, and let him win these rich bribes of Moab? Don't you think it means, "*I would like to go,* but I dare not."

There are people like that, seeing clearly the right, the will of God, and obeying, *not* because they love the right, but because they are afraid to go against it. Of course, that is a great deal better than disobeying. But it is not the best thing. The best thing is to feel sure that God's will is best, and to want to do it because it is the right. When one obeys unwillingly because he fears to disobey, there is danger of a fall like Balaam's.

At any rate, Balaam refused to do the wrong this time. Good for him if the temptation were over. But we are never safe from outside temptation. Our only safety is to make our hearts safe against yielding by giving them entirely to God. What was the next temptation? (*vv.* 15-17). A more honourable embassy, more tempting rewards. Then the evil of his heart shows itself. Did he not already know God's will? Would not a thoroughly honest-hearted man have promptly repeated his former answer? Did Balaam? No. He bade them tarry that night too, and for the sake of the high bribes for which he longed, he would try again if he could get leave to go with them.

What result? (*v.* 20). God gave him leave. That is a most puzzling verse. Do you think God's will had changed? I don't. I don't know how God's will was revealed to him. If through his conscience, I think I understand it. It is a thing that often happens to people. When they know the right, and are not satisfied to do it, they consider it all over again, dally with the temptation, look at its pleasant side, try if they cannot some way reconcile it with conscience. They try to wring the

185

consent of conscience to force God, as it were, to give them leave to go.

Do you notice anything very puzzling in *v.* 22? That God was angry at Balaam for going, while Balaam felt that he had got leave to go. That used to puzzle me when I was a child. I know better now by experience of my own conscience and that of others. I know you may wish something to be your duty, till you actually persuade yourself that it is. You can even kneel down and pray for guidance, and if your heart is firmly set on getting your own way, you may actually rise up almost believing that wrong is right, that God gives you leave to do it. What is the security against this? When you have to make a decision about duty, try to be honest with yourselves. Don't try to get your own way. Say, "Father, I am willing to do the thing I don't like if it be right." Remember our Lord's prayer, "Father, not My will, but Thine be done!"

§ 4. *Further Tricks with Conscience*

We continue the story. How grand and important Balaam felt with all this splendid cavalcade of chiefs and princes travelling as his escort. "What a superior person I am! how they all look up to me for guidance!" From *v.* 22 to 35 there is a very curious part of the story about Balaam's ass. It puzzles me. Some great scholars think it was a dream by which God spoke to him on the way. And in some ways it looks like it, for Balaam seems alone without the brilliant procession of princes that had started with him, and he does not seem in the least

186

surprised at this startling incident of the ass speaking. He takes it quite as a matter of course.

Did you ever notice how we all do that in dreaming? The most improbable things seem to us quite natural. So this incident looks very like what would happen in a dream. Some scholars think this whole section was inserted afterwards from another account. All through it the Divine name is Jehovah (THE LORD), whereas in all the rest of the narrative, except when repeating Balaam's own words, the historian uses the name "God" (Elohim). Other people say that this incident is as much part of the story as any other part, and there is no word in the chapter to hint that the narrator thought otherwise. And certainly there is no reason for doubting God's power to perform this miracle any more than all the other miracles. As the incident is so puzzling, and there is not time to deal with the whole chapter—we omit this section. The story pieces together quite smoothly without it if we pass from *v.* 21 to *v.* 36.

What an honourable reception Balaam got! Fancy a king coming to meet him to do him honour at the frontier city of his kingdom. No wonder he should feel proud and elated. But I don't think his conscience was quite easy, in spite of all his cleverness. Do you? Why not? Tell me exactly what he says to the king? (*v.* 38). "I have come, *but* I will not speak one word except what God allows." Does not it look like excusing himself to his conscience? It is a great soothing to one's conscience, when one is doing something wrong, to keep on reiterating and insisting that he will most certainly *not* do something else that is wrong. "I am going with bad companions, but I shall certainly not join them in their naughtiness and bad conduct." "It is true I am very careless about religion, but you will never find any hypocrisy about me." Oh, these tricks of conscience! Did you ever try them yourself? They are so easily learned, and they are so soothing and comforting on the evil road. Balaam had no business at all to be in the camp of Balak, except that he hoped something would enable him to earn his bribe. What a comfort to keep saying to himself that he certainly would not go beyond the word of the Lord!

What do you think is the lesson of this chapter? To beware of playing tricks with your conscience. Reverence conscience as God's messenger to you. Do everything you can to enlighten and educate it, by Bible-reading and prayer and right doing. Get the habit of listening to it and obeying. Every time you listen to its still small voice it will be plainer and clearer next time. Every time you shut your ears to its commands it will be lower and duller and more easily silenced next time.

Next chapter we continue the story, and find out the terrible result of Balaam's playing tricks with conscience.

NOTES

Vv. 20, 22. Would bear the rendering, "Since the men have come to call thee," and might mean, "Since through your own fault you have let them come back, have your own way; you may go with them, but beware what you say!" V. 22 clearly shows that the words imply no real willing permission for him to go.

V. 23, etc. I think the story of Balaam's ass is best dealt with as in the lesson. Let the pupil see the difficulty of the question, and that it is a perfectly legitimate position to say, "I do not know."

The teacher who has access to Bishop Butler's sermons should study his famous "Balaam" sermon.

QUESTIONS FOR LESSON XIX

Who were (1) Balaam, (2) Balak?

How does Balaam come into this story?

This is a study of conscience. How much do you know about conscience?

Show how Balaam played tricks with his conscience. Do people do that still? Give examples.

Was Balaam an entirely bad man? What was his fault?

What do you think of the story about Balaam's ass?

LESSON XX

BALAAM—A STUDY OF CONSCIENCE, PART II

Read Numbers XXIII., XXIV. 1-20.

Micah VI. 5-8.

2 Peter II. 15.

Revelations II. 14.

§ 1. Knowing Right and Doing Wrong

Recapitulate. Conscience. The tricks of conscience. What was Balaam's sin?

Last chapter ended with what scene? The meeting of the king and prophet at the frontier city. The stately royal procession waiting to welcome Balaam to Moab. How his heart would swell with pride at the sight of it, and at the sense of his own power. Yet do you think he was quite happy? Wonderful what a power conscience has of giving torment even in the midst of prosperity! I think the man was sad in the midst of all this grandeur. A much lower type of man would have been happier?

190

Why? Would have thrown over all thought of God and Right, which Balaam could not. A much higher type of man, such as Moses, would have been happier. Why? Because in his complete unselfishness and devotion to God he would have obeyed the promptings of conscience regardless of any consequences, and so have been quite happy. What was the great difference between the prophets Moses and Balaam? Moses lived for his people, his duty, his God; he was not proud of his gifts or power, nor ambitious of wealth and distinction for himself. Had he temptations and struggles like Balaam? Yes, and sometimes he fell, but his heart was so set on God and Right that he could not turn away from God— it would break his heart. Balaam had enough religion to make him miserable at his disobedience, not enough to make him glad and obedient. Have you ever known any one like that? Have you felt thus yourself?

There is a bit of the story not told here. I wonder if, after the grand procession, King Balak took the prophet aside to talk to him about his troubles. I wonder if this was the time when Balaam spoke the grand words which the prophet Micah tells of. (Read Micah vi. 5-8.) They are very grand words for Old Testament days—remind one of the words of our Lord Himself. Repeat them. "What doth the Lord require of thee, but to do justly, and to love mercy, and to walk humbly with thy God?" If we are right in reading these as Balaam's teaching to Balak, does it make his case still more sad, showing his high religious knowledge and his very low conduct? What lesson does it teach? That people may know and even feel deeply about religious truth without really carrying it into active exercise. They may know all the teaching of the Bible, and even at times be touched with the beauty and tenderness and unselfishness of our Lord's life, and yet be lazy and selfish and uncharitable and unloving. We must not mistake admiration of religion for religion itself.

§ 2. *Wishing Right and Doing Wrong*

Go on with story. Balaam, with his promptings of good and his longing after evil, is trying to win the Moabite reward—trying, in spite of his conscience again and again, to get God's permission to curse Israel. What is first done? Yes. Altars, sacrifices, Balaam prostrate alone before God on the mountain.

Ah! I think the wretched man's conscience and his guardian angel were struggling hard with him then. Oh, if he would but give up his evil worldly desires and yield gladly to God's will! The king is waiting by the altar, waiting impatiently for the prophet's return. He returns. What happens? Yes. The conscience and the guardian angel had nearly won that time. The Spirit of God within was too strong for his evil desires. I think the sight of that great host of God's people touched his heart. Perhaps the knowledge he had of Moses, the holy, righteous prophet of the Lord, made him long for better things himself. So—he can't resist the impulse—he lifts up his hands in blessing instead of cursing, and his poor, miserable heart goes out in that great craving—What? V. 10, "Let me die the death of the righteous," etc.

Ah, poor Balaam! He might have improved that

wish. How? "Let me *live the life* of the righteous"; that is the only way to die their death. Did he want to live that life? Ah! no. At least he is not willing to lose anything for it. He will try again with Balak and the altars, and try if he can't satisfy the king (*v.* 13).

What is the lesson? That mere wishing right is only a very little step forward. "Hell is paved with lazy wishes." Sometimes in novels one reads of worldly, self-indulgent, selfish people, with their pathetic sentiments and wishes after better things, and the author seems to think that this nearly makes up for their wrong-doing. Does it? Ah! no. These wishes come from God's Spirit, and *may* be the beginning of better things, but are utterly useless unless they rise up to *do*. The Prodigal might have sat for ever wishing among the pig-troughs if he had not said, *"I will arise and go."* Balaam wished to die the death of the righteous. We shall see by-and-by the death that he did die. Not the *wish*, but the *will*, not *feeling*, but *doing*, is what God looks for.

§ 3. *Victory of Conscience*

What is next effort? (xxiii. 14). Does it succeed? No. Blessing again. How angry and disappointed King Balak was! What does he ask now? (*v.* 25). "Neither curse them nor bless them." And still Balaam tries on to see if he can change God's will. You hear the same cry from him still: "I would not do wrong for the whole world, but am I quite sure that it is wrong?" Many outwardly religious people go on like that. Has God really forbidden it? Why should not I get on in the world? Why should not I get things I like? So they go on like Balaam, trying how far they can go. And over them all the time is the great, holy, unchanging God, with His eternal, unchanging laws of Right and Wrong.

So Balaam goes on. Again and again new altars are erected as he tried to change the Almighty's will. And now the final climax has come. He stands in the watcher's field at the top of Pisgah. Behind him lay the broad desert, stretching back to his Assyrian home. On his left the red mountains of Edom and Seir. Opposite, the rocky fortress of the Kenites, with the dim outline of the Arabian wilderness in the distance. And right below, the vast encampment of Israel—the nation whom he had come to curse.

And there as he stood, with his covetous desires and his struggling conscience, he felt like a whirlwind the prophetic power come upon him; he "heard the word of God, he saw the vision of the Almighty, falling into a trance, but having his eyes open." He seemed to see marvellous visions of the future. He saw Israel victorious over all its foes. And then in the far-away future he saw—but not now—he beheld, but not nigh, a Star rising out of Jacob, and a Sceptre out of the border of Israel, a vision, it may be, in that far-back age, of the coming of the Son of God to men. The Divine power within had, for the moment, overcome the sordid spirit of the man. "Blessed shalt thou be, Israel! Blessed is he that blesseth thee, and cursed is he that curseth thee!"

§ 4. Kept Back from Honour

So it seems as if the good in Balaam had conquered after all, spite of all his deceiving and tricking with conscience. Ah! good for Balaam if that were the end of the story. Can't you imagine the fierce anger of the king? Balak's anger was kindled against Balaam, and he smote his hands together. "I called thee to curse mine enemies, and, lo, thou hast blessed them altogether! Therefore now flee thou to thy place. I thought to promote thee to great honour; but, lo, Jehovah hath kept thee back from honour."

Well for Balaam if it were true. Well for us all if it were true, whenever honour depends on the sacrifice of principle, that we could say, "God and my conscience have kept me back from such honour." Can you give instances of such being true to-day? e.g. business man who refuses to get rich by tricks of trade. Statesman who for Right's sake is on unpopular side. Young man or woman who could have gay companions and frivolous amusements and be highly honoured amongst a set of godless companions. Boy or girl who might be a popular ringleader at school. But they have determined to live the true life. The Lord God has kept them back from honour—such honour as that.

§ 5. Utter Defeat

The story seems ended here. I wish it were. One feels so glad for poor Balaam just then, with the good side of his nature conquering—glad to see him bear to be turned disgracefully out of Balak's camp—perhaps turning in his downfall to Moses and telling him all his story. Perhaps that was when Moses learned it all.

But men who have lived most of their lives like Balaam, alas! do not quickly turn permanently to good. The next chapter tells of a terrible calamity and a terrible sin of Israel, which brought down on them the curse that all Balaam's divinations had failed to bring. They got tempted to join in the filthy idolatry of the Moabites, with all the horrible sin that followed in its train. And again, as before, God's punishment fell. "The chiefs of the people were hung up before the Lord, and a plague came out from the presence of the Lord that slew 24,000." What an awful punishment! What an awful sin! What an awful responsibility on those who tempted them to sin! But what has it all to do with Balaam, who had so conscientiously refused to curse them? Nothing, it would seem at first. Not a word about him in this chapter. But turn to chapter xxxi., after the punishment of the Moabites and Midianites who had seduced Israel into this terrible sin in order that God might curse them. There is just a passing mention of his name in the stern speech of Moses; but what an awful mention! (*v.* 16). These caused the children of Israel to trespass against the Lord *through the counsel of Balaam.* What a devilish thing! He could not go against God, but his soul was hankering still after the rewards of Moab. So when he had been turned out of Balak's camp, and his enthusiasm for righteousness had died away, he must have skulked back to the king one day: "I cannot disobey God, but I want to do what you wish. You want God's curse on them. I will counsel you how to draw them into a sin that will certainly curse them." And he did, and for that his name is held up to eternal shame wherever the Bible has reached. What does St. Peter call him? (2 Peter ii. 15). What does Book of Revelation say? (ii. 14).

You remember his wish, "Let me die the death of the righteous." What death did he die? (Numbers xxxi. 8). Slashed down amid the shrieking hordes of polluted Midian. That is the end. An awful, awful, miserable end.

§ 6. Lesson for Us

What is the great safeguard against such a life as Balaam's? The love of God and Right. The honest surrender of your heart to Christ. If Balaam had loved God he could not have asked for leave again and again to do wrong.

There are people still, conscientious people, too, whose rule of duty is the *minimizing rule* like Salaam's. "How little of God's will need I do—how much of self-pleasing may I practise without actually disobeying God and conscience?" Ah! it is a dangerous, dishonouring way—a poor, miserable, ungrateful way to treat God. Remember the grace of the Lord Jesus Christ, who, "though He was rich, yet for our sakes became poor." (2 Corinthians viii. 9). For our sakes was scoffed and beaten and spitted on and murdered, because He loved us. Let us pray for real love to Him in return. Thus shall we escape the danger of Balaam. Thus shall our conscience be kept undisturbed. Thus shall our service be loyal and true. Thus shall we "die the death of the righteous," and our last end be like his.

NOTES

V. 9, The people shall dwell alone. Point out how, while so many ancient peoples have been swept away and absorbed in the general mass of humanity, Israel still everywhere stands apart and "is not reckoned amongst the nations."

V. 14, Field of Zophim, to the top of Pisgah. Probably they were traversing the very ground that Moses traversed on that day when he went up to the top of Pisgah to die.

V. 24. Cf. Genesis xlix. 9.

Ch. xxiv. 14. Well for him if he *had* gone home "unto his people" and not stayed for his ruin. Some think that it was here, while "advertising" Balak of what should be, that he gave him the villainous advice about tempting Israel to fornication. One of the chief Jewish Targums, or commentaries, inserts that advice here. But I think it is very unlikely just when the man's conscience had, for the moment at least, been stirred to its depths.

V. 17, There shall come a Star, etc. The great Jewish Targums, or commentaries, interpret this as a prophecy of the Messiah. And this was evidently the reason why the false Messiah who appeared in the reign of the Emperor Adrian took the title *Bar-Cochab*, "the son of a star." See Ellicott's *Commentary*. I have not dealt with this subject, as I feared to distract attention from my central lesson on "Conscience."

QUESTIONS FOR LESSON XX

The prophet Micah records a fine saying of Balaam. What?

Tell me Balaam's wish about his death.

How only can a man die the death of the righteous?

Did Balaam live thus?

Now tell of the awful sin which ruined him.

What death did he die?

What does his story teach us?

LESSON XXI

THE THREE GREAT NATIONAL FESTIVALS

Read Deuteronomy XVI.

Refer to Exodus XXIII. 14-19.

Leviticus XXII. 34-43.

When Moses knew that he must never enter the Promised Land, and that very soon he must die in the wilderness and leave his people, he quietly began to prepare them for his departure. He had long talks with them, reminding them of God's care in the past, and pleading with them to be faithful and loyal when he was gone, and giving them directions for their future life in that land when he should be no more with them. I think it is very touching to see the old man standing before that crowd of people day after day, telling them how they were to worship God and thank Him for His goodness to them in the days to come in that beautiful new home of theirs, which he knew he should never share with them. We shall think of this more fully later on. The Book of Deuteronomy is the record of his last words to them, and we shall touch briefly on it as a whole. But it is necessary here to give in fuller detail one part of his directions—that about the Great Festivals which they must keep in Canaan.

Moses knew human nature well enough to see that it was necessary to keep some special annual celebrations to remind the nation of the past and of what they owed to God; else in a few centuries their descendants would be in danger of utterly forgetting. Just so the Christian Church appoints her great festivals, Christmas, and Easter, and Ascension, and Whitsuntide, to keep vividly before us the memory of the great facts of our religion.

How many were these festivals which Moses at God's inspiration commanded? Three. The feast of PASSOVER, the feast of PENTECOST, the feast of TABERNACLES.

§ 1. *The Passover*

We have already had a whole chapter devoted to this subject (*ch.* ix.), so little more is necessary to be said. The Passover should be distinguished from the other feasts. Though it, too, had some connection with the harvest (Leviticus xxiii. 10-14), yet it is not an agricultural feast, but a sacrificial, in memory of the great night of deliverance when the sprinkled blood saved the people. The references to the Passover in the Old Testament are not many (Joshua v. 10-12; 2 Chronicles xxx., xxxv; Ezra vi. 19). The lesson to be taught will be found in Lesson IX.

§ 2. Pentecost

Fifty days after the Passover wave sheaf (Leviticus xxiii. 10-14) was the Feast of Pentecost. Because it is seven weeks, i.e. a week of weeks, after the Passover, it is also called the Feast of Weeks (Exodus xxxiv. 22; Deuteronomy xvi. 10). What else is it called? The Feast of Harvest (Exodus xxiii. 16); and of Firstfruits (Numbers xxviii. 26). It lasted only a single day (Deuteronomy xvi. 9-12). It marked the completion of the *corn* harvest, not of the whole harvest, and therefore it can hardly be said to correspond to our Harvest Home, or Harvest Festival.

The real Harvest Festival of Israel was the Feast of Tabernacles. Pentecost marked only a certain stage in the ingathering, but the Feast of Tabernacles was for the combined produce of the whole year. "When thou hast gathered in thy labours out of the field." (See Exodus xxiii. 16; Leviticus xxiii. 39; Deuteronomy xvi. 13.)

The later Jews say that Pentecost also commemorated the giving of the Law on Mount Sinai, fifty days after the departure out of Egypt.

How were they to keep this festival? Sadly? No. Deuteronomy xvi. 11, "Thou shalt rejoice before the Lord thy God, thou, and thy son, and thy daughter, and thy servants, and the stranger, and the widow, and the fatherless that are among you." Is not that a lovely idea of religion, to rejoice and to make others rejoice? What a beautiful, happy world this would be if we all lived out our religion that way! They were to remember something sad. What? Deuteronomy xvi. 12, "Remember that thou wast a bondman in Egypt." I suppose that was to make them gladder and more grateful in the thought of the contrast with the happy, prosperous life in Canaan. Think of Moses as he reminded them that they had been bondmen in Egypt. I suppose the memory would rise in his heart of these old days and the sights of horror at the brick-fields and the day that he smote the Egyptian taskmaster dead in his anger. "Rejoice in the Lord," he says, "for all His goodness since that time."

§ 3. The Feast of Tabernacles

There was a bright, glad note of thanksgiving in the Feast of Pentecost, and even—though in a more subdued key—in the Feast of Passover. But the brightest, gladdest festival of the whole year was the Feast of Tabernacles. I think we may especially call it the Jewish Harvest Festival. The farm labours were over for the year; the harvest was gathered in. It was the feast of a nation resting from its work; the joyous feast amid the leafy boughs and the fresh-cut hay and the golden light of piled-up corn; "the feast of ingathering at the end of the year, when they had gathered in their labours out of the field."

It was evidently intended to be the most joyous festival of the year. See the fuller directions, Leviticus xxiii. 40: "Ye shall take you on the first day boughs of goodly trees, branches of palm-trees, and the boughs of thick trees, and willows of the brook; and ye shall rejoice before the Lord seven days." Why these boughs and branches? To make booths or tents of leaves over their heads to remind them of the sad time of wandering in the Wilderness, and so to deepen their gladness and thankfulness. It is just the same lesson as in the Feast of Pentecost, when they were bidden "remember when thou wast a bondman in Egypt," that thus they might more rejoice and thank God for their freedom. So now, with the happy homes and the rich, bountiful harvest of the good land that God had given, they were to rejoice in the memory of the dreary past which was over for ever.

So curious it looked—this dramatic reminder of the old desert life—coming in hundreds of years later in the surroundings of Jerusalem, so unlike the desert, with houses, and streets, and beautiful public buildings, and the Temple of God, stately and strong, in the place of the old movable Tabernacle of the Congregation.

Did they "rejoice in their feast," do you think? Aye, did they! "He who has not seen our Feast of Tabernacles," say the Rabbis, "does not know what joy means." Out from their houses and lodgings in Jerusalem they crowded into the Temple precincts, and booths were erected of palms and willows; and bunches of ripe fruit were hung over the booths, and the trumpets rang out, and the offerings were brought, and water and wine were poured out at the altar, and the people rejoiced praising the Lord. The desert life was over for ever; the harvest was safe; the corn was stored; the vintage was gathered. Blight and mildew, storm and rain, had done their worst and failed to break the ancient promise of God. Again had the earth brought forth her increase, and "God, even their own God, had given His blessing."

Probably every one of the Psalms which we sing at Harvest Festivals to-day were written by some inspired king or inspired farmer thousands of years ago for the national festivals, to express the people's gladness and thankfulness to God.

Don't you think it would do them good and make them love God, such a festival as that every year? Ah, poor Jews! I feel so sorrowful for them now. I (the writer) have seen, years ago, the poor creatures in my own city parish in their red brick artisan dwellings, trying so pathetically to keep up the memory of that old Feast of Tabernacles. It would bring tears into your eyes to think of the glorious old days and then to look at the few little dying branches of green stuff on the sheds in their back-yards, and the poor little efforts to keep the glad Feast of Tabernacles in the midst of a city that neither knew nor cared what they were doing.

I wonder if Moses, in his life beyond, was able to look down and rejoice with his nation in their joy long ago? And I wonder if he is able to see sorrowfully the poor little pathetic efforts in the city back streets to-day. I don't know. But I know that God sees and God cares. He hath not cast away His people.

I think of the Feast of Tabernacles in later days, when the Benjamites carried off wives from the vineyards of Shiloh (Judges xxi. 19); when Elkanah came up to Shiloh to worship (1 Samuel i. 3); when Solomon chose this festival for the dedication of his temple (1 Kings viii. 2); when Nehemiah read every day of the feast the words of the law of God (Nehemiah viii. 13-18). And there is one still more interesting.

Do you remember one very interesting Feast of Tabernacles at which our Lord was present? Where recorded? (John vii., viii.) I have referred already to some of the later ceremonies which were added in after days—the procession to Siloam to fetch water and pour it out solemnly at the altar. Amongst these later additions was also the lighting of the four great golden candelabra in the Court of the Women. You remember how our Lord spoke as He saw the water-drawing on "the Great Day of the Feast" (John vii. 37), "If any man thirst, let him come unto Me, and drink." And again, probably at the lighting of the Great Candelabra (John viii. 12), "I am the Light of the world," etc.

§ 4. *The Four Lessons*

What are the four definite directions given by God about these national festivals for worship?

(1) That all the men should come at the appointed times (Exodus xxii. 17).

(2) That all should worship together (Deuteronomy xvi. 5-7).

(3) That they should rejoice (Deuteronomy xvi. 11-14).

(4) That they should come prepared to give (Deuteronomy xvi. 16).

Let each child repeat these and show in the chapter where they are enjoined.

§ 5. Lesson One: Public Worship

Now let us see what lessons for us about God's will are here. (1) How many of the men of Israel were ordered to come? Was any single one at liberty to stay away from this public worship and thanksgiving to God? Not one.

If any man of Israel who was not sick or prevented by something of vital importance were absent, don't you think God would regard it as a sin and disrespect shown to Him? Many of the women came too. Our Lord's parents both went (Luke ii. 41). But the order was not made strictly about them. Why, do you think? In so many cases it would be almost impossible for a woman to leave her household and little children when her husband was away, and to be away for days, or weeks together in Jerusalem. So the women went when they could. But the men could not avoid going under penalty of sin against God.

What is the lesson for us? Surely the bounden duty of the public worship of God. The *duty* I say. There is also the great *loss* to the spiritual life of any one who neglects public worship. But the lesson before us is plainly of the *duty* of it. God's will is surely the same now as then, and to dishonour Him by neglecting public worship must be a grave sin. What man may absent himself now? Not one. Do you think women may do so now? God is very loving and considerate, and if a poor woman has young children and, *sorely against her will,* is unable to be often in church, God would be gentle with her and bless her in spite of it. But remember the Jewish woman had to go a long journey and be away weeks together. Therefore the same excuse does not apply. If necessary she should ask her husband or a neighbour or friend to stay in the house for one service at least. Unless she is doing her best about it she is not free from the sin.

Do you think "all the males" in our country obey God in this? Oh, it is awful, this sin, and it is growing worse in England, and the men are worse than the women. I wish all our children were differently taught about this. I wish our pulpits would frequently insist that it is not merely a fault or a failing or a loss, but a great SIN of disrespect to God. With all their errors of teaching, the Roman Catholic clergy do insist on this. From childhood their people are taught the obligations of public worship and the great sin of neglecting it. And the result is most remarkable. It is a wretched confession to have to make that the neglect of public worship is far more amongst Protestants than amongst Roman Catholics. A clergyman told the writer lately that not 10 per cent. of the people in his district came to church, and the accounts from parishes with large numbers of working men are perfectly awful. Unless our nation repent of it, and mend its ways, God's blessing cannot remain with us.

People say sometimes, "I can pray as well at home." Do you think that will do as well? I fear those who talk thus don't pray much at home or anywhere else;

but even if they did pray at home, would that suffice? Remember the worship of God is not merely the asking in private of what we want, each for himself, but the public kneeling with His people to offer Him gratitude and praise and adoration. Do your best to help against this national sin. Pray for God's grace to keep you clear of that sin yourselves, and do all you can to urge others to keep clear of it.

§ 6. Lesson Two: Unity

There is not room to say much about this here. But notice how especially these Jews were ordered to have a *united worship.* They were not allowed to say, "We will separate into groups and worship when and where we like. It does not matter if we are worshipping God." No. "Keep together in your great acts of worship," said Moses. And Moses said it, remember, by God's inspiration. Unity was of vital importance to them as a Church, and as a nation, to accomplish God's purposes.

Is it not the same with the Christian Church? Don't you think our Lord sent out His Church to accomplish a great purpose? Do you think it will do just as well if split up into 100 separate sects—separate in worship, separate in work—sometimes even hostile to each other? Never mind who is to blame for the present state of things. Enough to know that it is making religion a mockery. Think about the need of this unity for the work Christ has set us. Pray about it. Help towards it all you can. Remember our Lord's great prayer for it

(John xvii. 21), "That they all may be one . . . that the world may believe that Thou hast sent Me."

§ 7. Lesson Three: Rejoice

There is another important lesson. (See *vv.* 11-14.) *Thou shalt rejoice.* That was the direction given 3000 years ago to the old Jewish Church for their religious services. And I think it would be a good thing for us in these days to remember it more. We are a much less joyous-hearted people. We have less of the joyful child-spirit in our religion. We older people, at any rate, do not make it the glad thing we ought.

And I doubt if even children do it either as you should. What happens when you kneel down in the morning and at night? Try to remember. Do you feel glad like children who trust, and rejoice in the kind, loving, considerate heart of your Father in heaven? Do you say, "Lord, I am glad that I am going out into my life to-day in Your presence. You like to see me happy. You will be glad when I try to be good"? Or do you, as you solemnize your thoughts to kneel down, do you feel a bit afraid and shrinking and a trifle sad, and do you sometimes feel a wee bit of relief when it is all over and you can rush off to romp with your brothers and sisters or to rush out into the sunshine? If so, don't you think it is rather hard on God (I say it reverently) to have to bear this? Don't you think your father or mother would feel it hard if you felt thus about meeting them? And God has to bear that so often from us, and to say nothing about it. He says, "My child, thou shalt rejoice in thy religion, thy prayers, thy thanksgivings." But we do not—much. And I think God is sorrowful for it. He goes on still blessing and helping us and making us happy and good just the same as if we rejoiced in Him. But don't you think He would like it if there were more joy and trust shown by us? Do you think poor little insignificant creatures like us could give joy to the great Almighty God? Our Lord says, Yes. (Luke xv. 1-10). There is joy in heaven and joy in the angels when men turn to God. I think there would be joy in heaven, too, if we showed more joy on earth at coming into God's presence like the Israelites. Do you think God deserves it of us? Do you think it would make life and religion brighter and happier? Will you try and think about it?

§ 8. Lesson Four: Giving

"Thou shalt not come before the Lord empty." In our lesson about the Tabernacle we saw the importance of this. Not that God needs our gifts, but that He delights to see us show our gratitude thus, and for that reason He has left His greatest works—the support of his Church, the care of the poor, the Missions to the heathen, etc.—entirely dependent on our effort. If we refuse to help, these must suffer. Let us, then, give gladly, "not grudgingly or of necessity, for God loveth a cheerful giver."

QUESTIONS FOR LESSON XXI

What were the three great national festivals of Israel?

What time of the year was each?

What did each commemorate?

Which was the harvest festival?

Did our Lord ever come to any of these festivals?

Why did God desire that all should come to these services?

What is their lesson for us about (1) public worship, (2) joyful religion, (3) giving for God's service?

THE LONELINESS OF HIS OLD AGE

Read Numbers XX. 23 to XXI. 10;

also XX. v. 1.

§ 1. Miriam's Death

I think the story of Moses' life grows more and more touching and pathetic as it draws towards its close. Last chapter told of the deep sorrow and disappointment that followed his sin, a sorrow and disappointment that seemed to purify his life and draw him nearer to the God who had sent him the sorrow.

Now I see the sadness and loneliness deepening. While they waited at Kadesh, probably after the time of his sin in smiting the rock, Miriam died, and Josephus says Moses mourned for her thirty days, and that the people took part in her great public funeral. Don't you think Moses would miss her, and be lonely without her? You see his was a lonely life at his best. His high position made him lonely, the great difference in character between him and his people would make it worse. I think he would greatly feel Miriam's death. You remember her first appearance? (Exodus ii. 4). Surely he would often think of the story of that wise little sister who had taken care of him in the bulrushes and managed so tactfully with Pharaoh's daughter. Perhaps she had been with him to encourage him when he made his great life decision to leave the Palace in Egypt for the slave huts in the brick-fields. She had led the women in the glad *Te Deum* of victory at the Red Sea, and she had been with him in all his struggles and all his glory since the Exodus, and except on one occasion, when her feminine jealousy of another woman was roused (Numbers xii. 1), she seems to have been a true and faithful helper. Zipporah seems to have been long dead. I wonder where the two sons were? The old chief seems always so alone. His sister's death would surely make this worse.

§ 2. Aaron's Death

And scarce was she laid in the grave when another bereavement came. What? Did he know it was coming? Yes. Aaron had been included with himself in the sentence of exclusion from the Promised Land. But probably he did not know it would be so soon. Where was the camp now? (xxi. 22). What brought it here? Another disappointment about getting into Canaan. Edom would not let them pass, so they had to turn another way to try. During this time God's direction about Aaron came to Moses. What was it? Aaron's time had come to die. He was to have a grand death. "Take Aaron and Eleazar his son up into Mount Hor; and strip Aaron of his priestly garments, and put them on Eleazar his son, and Aaron shall die there."

Another of the grand features of which the story is so full. The central figure, the aged high priest in his beautiful robes walking feebly up the mountain with Moses and Eleazar, going away from his people for ever. He had loved and worked for them. Yes, and he had grievously sinned with them more than once! (Exodus xxxii.; Numbers xii. 1). What do you think of him now that he is about to go out of our story? Yes, he had shown weakness, cowardice, jealousy, but how often? Do you think it fair to judge his life by these few isolated acts? As you read the whole story—how he had been Moses' helper and spokesman in that long struggle with Pharaoh, and on the whole Moses' faithful comrade all through the lonely desert life—don't you think the trend and direction of his life was towards God? He was a man very inferior to Moses, but I feel sure he was a humble struggler after God.

Don't you think it was with a sorrowful heart that his great brother walked up beside him that day—with a sorrowful heart he looked into his face as he stripped off him one by one his garments of glory and beauty to invest his son and successor in the priesthood? And then as he waited amid the great cliffs as the days passed till death came and he laid in the grave his brother and comrade and friend—don't you think he was sorrowful and lonely?

Then see him return to that troublesome leadership—alone—alone—more lonely than he had ever been in his lonely life.

§ 3. *The Loneliness of Old People*

I wonder if young people can understand that one of the chief sorrows of old age is that gradually increasing feeling of being alone? As the years go by the friends of our youth drop off one by one and leave us more and more companionless. And as we get older we don't make new friends easily. Acquaintances—yes. Friends—no. The friends that most people value most are the old friends they have made in their younger days when the heart was fresh and green.

It is one of the things that should curb mere worldly ambition. It is God's will for us all to be ambitious, to do good work and get to the top of the tree if we can. But if a man does it merely for the praise and gratification of his friends and comrades, it is so sad when he reaches the top to find most of them gone. The true high ambition to be noble and faithful and good is not saddening, for it goes on into the Unseen Life with us where the old comrades are and we have it and them for ever. But mere worldly ambition for success in order to be praised of men is very disappointing.

I think, too, there is a great difference between the old age of mere worldly people, with no high desires, and the old age of the strugglers after God and good. Both are a bit lonely, but the latter are peacefully lonely, with a deep interest in the life to come, and eager looking forward to it, to get their puzzles answered, to meet their dear ones, to look into the face of Christ. I (the writer) am thinking just now of a distinguished man whom I know; very old and very famous. His highest ambitions have been realized. He has got fully to the "top of the tree." But he told a friend of mine one day lately how lonely it was. No wonder. The dear young wife who had been his comrade in his early struggles, and who was so proud of him, was gone, and his honours had lost most of their value since she was not by to share them. All his closest old friends are gone. He entered into the high reward of his life-work too late—alone. Thank God that he was able to add that across the river of death are waiting for him most of those whom he loved the best. Across the Unseen is the goal of his life.

§ 4. How God Prepares His Children for Bed

Thus God deals with us all as life goes by. Is it hard on us, do you think? I think it would be but for the fair life beyond. As it is I think it is *God's kind way of making it easier and pleasanter to us to go away into that life beyond.*

It is, I think, like a little child tired out by its birthday party, tired out and needing sleep; but the comrades are not gone, and the toys are spread about, and it seems so hard to be told to go to bed. But by-and-by the children go home, and the toys one by one are put away, and the lights are being put out through the house as mother takes the weary little boy to his cot. It is easy to go now, especially if he knows that the morning, when it comes, will bring back to him the toys and the friends again. Thus I think God was preparing Moses for his going to sleep, and thus He is preparing old people that you and I know. He is letting them lose the old comrades and the interests that filled up the busy earthly day, till at last they are willing to go to sleep in the glad hope of awaking in the morning in the Life Beyond with the old comrades waiting, and the new blessed unselfish life interests for all eternity. Does it seem so hard to you now that God lets them grow lonely?

§ 5. *The Brazen Serpent*

Read Numbers XXI. 4-10.

We cannot pass over this incident, if only on account of our Lord's reference to it. What? (John iii. 14). Where had Aaron died? Now they were moving on after his death, going round the border of Edom to find another entrance to Palestine. What were their feelings? (*v.* 4). Discouraged by reason of the way. It was a depressing time for them, and surely much more so for Moses—why? Death of Aaron and Miriam—sentence of exclusion from Palestine, etc.

Once more we have the old familiar cry of the murmuring against God. It is a comfort that this is the last time in this story. I think the new generation was much better than the old, who had by this time nearly all died in the wilderness. What was the cry now? What punishment? Travellers say that this part of the desert is infested with poisonous serpents. They were now allowed to increase more than usual and became very dangerous; so that the people lived in terror, never knowing when they might touch or tread on one of the venomous creatures. "Fiery" probably refers to the burning inflammation of the bite.

So they repented again. I wonder if they ever repented except when they were hurt? What did God tell Moses to do? Was it not a much simpler way than to give each one medicine or send a doctor to each? And all could have the remedy. It only needed looking up. How could this cure anyone? Just because God chose to attach the cure to it. The wounded people just believed God's word and looked up and at once were cured.

Our Lord uses the story as a beautiful type of what? How is it so? What is the venomous disease in us? Did you ever feel it in you? At what times specially? What is the Divine cure for the ill temper and disobedience and wrong of every kind? Every time you feel it, go and kneel down and think of the Blessed Lord hanging bleeding on the Cross for us and for our sins. Look up to Him and say, "Lord, who wast lifted up to heal us—heal me!" Do you understand fully how this cures you? Did the Israelites understand fully? Just like them—we look up and beseech Him earnestly to make us whole and trust Him to do it. He cares far more than we do about the result.

QUESTIONS FOR LESSON XXII

Another death in Moses' family. Whose?

Who else of the family had died not long before?

Make picture in words of Aaron's death.

What makes life more lonely as people grow old?

What is the teaching of that picture in this lesson, about tired child going to bed?

Tell the story of the brazen serpent.

Tell of our Lord's reference to this.

LESSON XXIII

PREPARING FOR THE END

Read Deuteronomy XXXI.

§ 1. Was Moses' Life a Failure?

We are now drawing to the close of the history of Moses. An old man, lonely, disappointed, suffering for his own fault. Do you think it a prosperous, satisfactory close?

There are many people in the world who think that happiness and prosperity and gratified ambition are the great boon to be desired as the result of a life. I'm afraid it is the commonest notion. We see it in the usual stories for children and the novels for grown-up people. In these the good child, in the end, gets all the nice things, the faithful lovers are happily married, the good people end their lives in comfort and prosperity, every one that deserves good receives his good in full *earthly* measure. Do you think that is what always happens in real life? I do not. I do think that all who deserve good do receive good, but not always in mere *earthly* measure and of mere *earthly* things. What do I mean by that? Yes. God has much nobler rewards for a faithful life than earthly success and money and high position, and nice carriages and servants. God does not seem to think these the chief good for men. What does God think the very best thing for us? High character, that we should be faithful and brave and unselfish and good. For it is only that type of person that can enjoy the delight of the endless life to come. You see the joy of that life will be the joy of character, the joy of goodness, the joy of likeness to the nature of God, the sort of pure beautiful pleasure that comes to a boy or girl now after doing kindly, unselfish, helpful things at cost of trouble and deprivation to themselves. So, naturally, in God's sight the highest reward of a beautiful life is a beautiful character, the most satisfactory close does not consist of riches and position and fine carriages and servants. Why? Because they must all be left behind at death. The most satisfactory close of a life consists in the fitness it has gained for all the continued life of love to God, and beautiful, unselfish service of others for all eternity.

So now I ask your opinion again about the end of Moses' life? Instead of dying in great honour and glory a mighty king, with an adoring nation at his feet, as some of us think he deserved, we see him going to his death alone, without friend or child or wife beside him—with God's chastisement upon him. So I ask your opinion, was it a satisfactory close to his life, or was his life a failure? Do you think any man ever went away into the new life beyond the grave more fitted for a glorious, happy future? We shall see more about that new life of his in the next chapter. We now go on with the story.

§ 2. Preparing for the End

The wars of Moses were over. He had conquered the tribes that barred the way to Palestine. He had led the people to the border of the land over which he must not pass. And now the time must come that he must die. Not quite of old age, for "his eye was not dim nor his natural force abated." (xxxiv. 7). Why, then, must he die? (See Numbers xxvii. 12-14.) The Lord had said to him, "Get thee up into Mount Abarim, and see the land; and when thou hast seen it, thou shalt be gathered to thy fathers; thou shalt not go over thither, for ye rebelled against My commandment in the desert of Sin, in the strife of the congregation, to sanctify Me at the water before their eyes."

Humbly and obediently the old man bowed to that decree, though it deprived him of the dearest wish of his life. Read all through his closing words—no grumbling nor repining. His grand faith in God rose superior to all. He knew that he was punished justly, and that it was best for him to be punished, that whatever God did must certainly be best. A beautiful spirit in which to die.

For months before he had been looking forward to his death, preparing the people for it, talking and teaching and advising them. Where do you find all this? All the Book of Deuteronomy is his touching series of discourses in these solemn days when the people knew the end was drawing nigh. I wish we could go over those discourses together—like the advice of a father to his children, like the farewell sermons of a very loving, earnest pastor to his people. I think they must often have brought tears into these people's eyes. He recounted the whole story of their wanderings, and showed how good God had been to them. And they would not forget the Lord their God, but love Him and cleave to Him always, and renounce idolatry and impurity and wickedness of every kind. Oh, how eagerly and passionately he pleads with them, and then how solemnly he warns them! "See," he says, "I have set before thee this day life and good, death and evil; in that I command thee to love the Lord thy God, and to walk in His ways; that the Lord thy God may bless thee in the land whither thou goest in to possess it." Oh, I think they are such noble, beautiful, touching words, these last discourses of Moses! If I knew nothing of his story before, these pleadings alone would make me love and admire him.

§ 3. *What He Did on His Last Birthday*

Now, on the last birthday of his life (how do you know it was his birthday? How old was he?) he calls his dear people together again for his last words. There are three things especially he wants to talk about. What are they? (*vv.* 1-14).

(1) FAREWELL—He fears they will be cowards again, as in the day of the spies, so he advises them. Don't be frightened or distrustful. Don't fear your enemies. God is with you. As He has been with you all my time so He will be when I am gone (*vv.* 1-6).

(2) THE NEW LEADER—Then he gives a solemn charge to the man who was to succeed him as leader.

Who was it? I think he must always have wished and hoped this. He seemed so to love and trust Joshua and keep him near him, his young lieutenant and friend. And do you remember his first prayer when God sentenced him to die without entering the land? (See Numbers xxvii. 12-18.) I think it was a relief and pleasure to him when God answered him by naming Joshua. He could trust Joshua as he could trust no other man. When we read on in the next volume of this series we shall see how worthy of trust Joshua was. But now the old chief is going away from them all for ever, and he knows, from his own experience, how much Joshua will have to bear, and what dangers are lying before him. So, after his farewell to the people, Moses called Joshua, the son of Nun, and said to him, in the sight of all Israel, "Be strong and of good courage, for thou must go with this people into the land. . . . And the Lord He it is that doth go before thee. He will be with thee. He will not fail thee, nor forsake thee, fear not, neither be dismayed." Is it not touching to see what a perfect trust he had in God? I wish we could all have such!

(3) THE BIBLE—But there is something else to do still on this great last birthday of his—what? (*vv.* 9-14). To provide for the safe keeping of "the Book of the Law," the first written part of our present Bible. I don't quite know how much is meant by "this Book of the Law." (The common opinion is that the Five Books of Moses, Genesis to Deuteronomy, were all written by him exactly as they stand. But many scholars believe that what Moses left was not this complete work, but only the kernel or part of it and that it was completed

and edited by later writers in the Jewish Church. It does not greatly matter. Here we leave it an open question.) Find me some of the passages where we can see Moses writing the beginning of the Bible? (See Exodus xvii. 44; xxxiv. 27; Deuteronomy xxxi. 19-24.) During these forty years this thinker and writer, who had been brought up "in all the wisdom of the Egyptians," kept his book of records written on parchment or on skins, and probably retained in his own custody. Now some other guardians must be provided. Who? Where was it to be kept? (*v.* 24). Yes, the Priests and the lay elders or princes should be in charge of it, and keep it in the side of the ark. Probably there were many copies of it for use in reading to the people. How were these to be kept from error and corruption? (*vv.* 10-12). At end of every seven years, at the Feast of Tabernacles, they were to hear the whole book recited. Don't you think it was a good plan? Eight hundred years afterwards, in evil days, when Israel was neglecting its Bible, and this Book of Moses had been forgotten and lost, we have an interesting account of how Hilkiah, the priest, found it again (2 Kings xxii. 8-13), and also of a wonderful Feast of Tabernacles in later days, where we see Moses' command exactly fulfilled by Ezra (Nehemiah viii. 2, 3).

§ 4. His Death-Song

Are these the last words of Moses? No. After the great last birthday in the days yet remaining before he should go up to die, solemn thoughts were in the old man's heart, and burst forth in lofty poems to be kept by Israel for ever.

Do you remember how we saw the writing of poems was part of the higher education of the young nobles in Egypt? From all we know of Moses we may well believe he excelled in this. What earlier poem of his have we? (Exodus xv.) The grand *Te Deum* for their salvation from Egypt. Now we have the two fine poems as he was leaving the world. It is said that the swan, when dying, sings her beautiful death-song, and Dean Stanley (History of Jewish Church) calls these the swan-song of Moses. Of course, they ought to be printed in poetical form. The first is "THE SONG OF THE ROCK," praising God, who was their Rock and Defence. We can only just look at it now in chap. xxxii. And then the "BLESSING OF THE TRIBES" (chap. xxxiii.). Ah! their faithful, loving old friend cannot go without blessing them. He seems to forget all their cruelty and ingratitude and rebellion against him, and how their murmurings had been the cause of his being shut out of the land. He forgets everything but that they are his people committed to him by God, and that he wants God to bless them before he dies. Is it not a beautiful close to a noble life! Don't you feel more and more sure of our decision at the beginning of this lesson that, in spite of all seeming failure, his life was a grand success, and that he went away into the Unseen Life gloriously fitted for the unselfish activities of the future! God give us all such a life and death as his!

QUESTIONS FOR LESSON XXIII

Now Moses is about to die. Tell some of the sorrow of his old age.

Do you think his life was a failure? Why not?

What does real success in life mean? Money? Fame? Pleasure? What?

Is any good man's life a failure?

What three things did Moses speak of on his last birthday before his death?

What did he direct about the early beginnings of the Bible?

LESSON XXIV

THE PASSING OF MOSES AND HOW HE RETURNED FROM THE UNSEEN

§ 1. Preparation for Death

I have called this the "Passing of Moses." I think it was more a passing than a death. We have read of the old chieftain's closing days, his faithfulness to God, his affectionate anxiety for the people, his touching farewell to them and their new leader, and how he blessed them with an old man's dying benediction.

And then, almost like the Blessed Lord Himself, "as he blessed them he was parted from them and carried up into"—not heaven—not yet—that cannot be for him until Christ comes for him and for us—but into the fair Waiting Life in the dim Unseen Land where all the great saints and heroes of the past, and all our own dear ones, departed in Christ, though they be perhaps neither saints nor heroes, are waiting, waiting always the second coming of our Lord.

Do you think he knew much about the Hereafter life? We find scarcely any reference to it in his story. It is only our Lord who has fully revealed it. Perhaps it was so important for the Jews to think of God as the living God, the God who was so close to man in this life, a part which we do not think of enough. I don't know. But, anyway, I feel sure that the man who lived so close to God's presence all these years would know as well as we do that death was not the end of his intercourse with God.

I picture him to myself, after blessing the people, quietly returning to his tent for the last time, to spend his night in thoughts of God, or preparing himself for the great event of the morrow—going up into the mountain to die. Have you ever heard people talk of "preparing for death"? Do you think Moses needed much preparing? Ah! I think it is only those accustomed to turn their thoughts much to God during life that can easily do it in preparation for death. I (the writer) have often seen people who have been neglecting prayer and Bible and communion with God all their lives—and, oh, it is a dreary, discouraging thing to see them trying to think of such things when death approaches. It is so irksome and distasteful to them. God is such a stranger to them. And I have seen others whom it was a delight to talk to as death drew near, and the eager eyes looked forward with glad hope to meeting our Lord and the dear ones departed. When should be our preparation for death? All our life, as in Moses' case. First, be sure that there is a true surrender of your life to our Lord to be His soldiers and servants to your lives' end. Try to get the fixed habit of spending some little time, at least every morning and evening, alone with God, reading something about Him in His Word, talking to Him of your failures and your sins, and your longing to be good, and thanking Him for His mercy and love in the beautiful hope He has given you in this world and the next. When you are older have your regular fixed times for Holy Communion, re-consecrating your life and receiving that Divine strength which Christ conveys through that Blessed Sacrament. Then, as life goes on, God will seem very near to you, and life will be beautiful and faithful and unselfish, and death will be very easy and happy as it was to Moses.

§ 2. Weeping Too Late

Many thrilling pictures have come before us in this history, but surely this last one is the most thrilling of all.

I don't think even the young children who crowded out of the tents that morning would ever forget, all the days of their life, that day when the great loving leader and father of his people went up out of their sight alone to die. Do you think they were sorry? (See *v.* 8), "the days of weeping and mourning." Josephus, the Jewish historian, says, "he withdrew from the camp amid the tears of the people, the women beating their breasts, and the children crying with uncontrolled weeping." Don't you like to see them, loving and crying for him, even then? Ah! there are many like them still. All the days of his life amongst them they were breaking his heart with their petulance and ingratitude, and now, as he is going to his death, they see at last how good and how lovable he was. If he could have come back then I think they would have tried to be good to him.

Do you think that ever happens now? I am afraid I have sometimes seen it, the sobbing and lamenting, and the loving words engraved on the tombstone at the close of a life that has been lived all its days unthanked and unappreciated. Is there anyone in your home that you might have thus to cry for? Examine yourselves. Often we thoughtlessly neglect our own relatives more than strangers.

> "We have pleasant words for the strangers
>   And smiles for the passing guest,
> But we hurt our own by look and tone
>   Though we love our own the best."

Yes! we do often really love them the best, but we don't find it out sometimes till after they are dead. And then we cry our hearts out, and say on our knees, "O God, if I had her back for one day to tell her that I loved her!" Will you think of this at your prayers to-night, and thank God if they are still with you, and tell them you love them, and resolve to be good to them, and make them happy, without waiting till they die?

§ 3. The End—On Earth

So Moses goes away—upward—upward; and the great weeping host follow him with their eyes, from ridge to ridge, from terrace to terrace, to the rocky

232

range of Moab, to the high places of
of the watchers on the top of Pisgah. H⌣
going up that lonely mountain, without eve⌐.
close his eyes! And yet he is not alone, for the .
is with him, the Father who loves him, who in lov⌐.
discipline is punishing him to-day.

What solemn thoughts would rise within him as
he goes up, as he looks back on his strange chequered
life-path, from the home of his boyhood in Pharaoh's
palace to the lonely mountain on which he must die
to-day, the life-path so wisely and lovingly guarded for
him by God.

Now he is nearing the summit, the peak of Nebo.
Beneath him with bursting heart he can see the white
tents of Israel, his children whom he loved and carried
on his heart for forty years. He and they shall meet no
more on earth. He turns his eyes away. And as he does
so a beautiful sight appears before him. The blue hills
and broad spreading valleys of Palestine, the good land
and large, the land of his day-dreams for forty years
and more. He saw it with his eyes but must not go over
thither.

Now comes the end. We cannot follow him farther—
he passes from view as he reaches the cloud-capped
summit to be alone with God in the grand solitudes
of the mountains. Who can imagine the solemnity of
that hour! The Jews have a beautiful old legend about
it—how the Angel of Death approached him, but drew
back in terror as he saw the light of God shining on his
face. "I may deepen Gehenna into a lower depth, but

over the son of Amram I cannot prevail. His face is like that of a seraph in the heavenly chariot—his visage is shining with the radiance of God." Again he approached him, but he dared not strike. Then Moses stood up in prayer, and cried, "O Lord of the universe, who wast revealed to me in the Burning Bush—remember that Thou didst carry me up into Thy presence forty days and forty nights—have mercy upon me; hand me not over to the Angel of Death!" And his prayer was answered, for He who ruleth in the highest heavens Himself stooped down to receive the soul of Moses. The Almighty with a Divine kiss received his soul. As it is written (Deuteronomy xxxiv. 5), "Moses, the servant of the Lord, died by the mouth of the Lord."

But the Bible gives no warrant for any fanciful stories. With silent reserve it only tells us this: "Moses, the servant of the Lord, died there in the land of Moab over against Bethpeor, but no man knoweth of his sepulchre unto this day." That is all we know. At the moment of his death God and he were alone together. No hand of man closed his eyes. No human implement dug his grave. In some sense that we can never know

> "The Angels of God upturned the sod,
> And laid the dead man there."

That was the grandest funeral that ever passed on earth,
To lie in state while angels wait and the taper stars
    gleamed forth,
And the dark rock pines like the tossing plumes
    over his bier to wave,
And God's own hand in that lonely land to lay him
    in his grave.

O lonely grave in Moab's land, O dark Bethpeor's hill,
Speak to these curious hearts of ours and teach them
    to be still,
God hath His mysteries of grace—ways that
    we cannot tell,
He hides them deep like the hidden sleep of him
    He loved so well.

§ 4. His Life after Death

So at last we have come to the end of Moses' life. Have we? Ah! no, only of the first great chapter of it—the part of it lived here.

Side by side with this life runs the mysterious Unseen Life where far the greater part of God's great Church is to-day, living and loving and waiting for His coming. At the moment of death we enter it. We see others in it. We can recognize them in it. Remember what our Lord told the dying thief as they were both about to pass over its border together, "To-day thou shalt be with Me," which surely means, "This day we shall meet at the other side and recognize each other as the two men who hung together on Calvary." Think of the countless millions in that Waiting Land. Paradise is not the final Heaven, but it is, as it were, the courtyard of Heaven. It is not the Palace of the King, but, as it were, the precincts of the Palace. And St. Paul said, when he expected to go there "unclothed"—without the body, that he expected to be "with Christ" (Philippians i. 23).

I think all the wonder and beauty of what Moses saw from the mountain just before his passing away was as nothing to that which he saw a few minutes after it. The Sadducees thought he was dead with Abraham and Isaac and Jacob. How did our Lord correct them? God, He says, calls Himself their God long after they had passed from earth. He would not do so if they were dead, for "God is not the God of the dead, but of the living." (Mark xii. 27).

I think of Moses closing his eyes on Mount Nebo. I think of them opening in a few minutes on a "light that never was on sea or land." I think what gloriously unselfish work would be given there to a man so gloriously unselfish. I think how he would learn the full meaning of the law at Sinai and the Blood sprinkling and the Day of Atonement.

Do you think this is all mere idle guessing? Do you think we can know nothing about it since no one has come back to tell us? It is not so. Did not this man come back? When? Where? On the Mount of Transfiguration (Matthew xvii. 3; Luke ix. 30) to talk with our Lord "of His decease which He should accomplish at Jerusalem." Don't you think then he had learned in the meantime more about the Atonement and the Blood sprinkling that pointed to Christ?

It gives one such a curious feeling this following Moses into his new life. It is like "going to the end of the world and looking over the wall." I wish I could really look over that wall in the long years after Moses passed in! How eagerly he and the other great waiting souls must have been watching the events of the Redemption! How gladly he came out to talk with Christ "of His decease which He should accomplish at Jerusalem." With what joyful worship they would meet our Lord when "He descended into Hades." How wonderful to see this man Moses who long ago on earth had been admitted into the counsels of God—to see him still admitted into these high counsels in the Waiting Land. How else should he come out to confer with his Lord about the Crucifixion in Jerusalem?

Would it not be nice if we could continue our study of his life, and have further sets of chapters, "Moses' Life in the Unseen"? We cannot. Why? We have not the materials *yet. Yet.* Some day we shall. There may be some who have begun with us these chapters about Moses here on earth, and who have since passed into the Waiting Land and learned perhaps very wonderful things about the rest of his story there, things which the writer of these pages was unable to tell them. For remember we are talking of a living man—a man whom we shall ourselves probably see some day when we go into that mysterious land and ask questions of what has puzzled us, and meet those gone before us "whom we have loved long since and lost a while."

QUESTIONS FOR LESSON XXIV

Do you think Moses needed much preparation for death? What is the best preparation for death?

Picture in words that touching, sorrowful scene of Moses' departure from his people.

Does anybody know about his actual death or his grave?

Could you repeat any part of Mrs. Alexander's poem, "The Death of Moses"?

Is Moses dead now? Once he came back to earth to meet our Lord. When?